Sierra de Aracena

– a Walk! Guidebook

by

David & Ros Brawn

DISCOVERY WALKING GUIDES LTD

Sierra de Aracena - a Walk! Guidebook
First Edition - September 2004

Copyright © 2004

Published by
Discovery Walking Guides Ltd
10 Tennyson Close, Northampton NN5 7HJ,
England

Maps
Maps are adapted from **Sierra de Aracena Tour &
Trail Map** (ISBN 1-899554-97-1) published by
Discovery Walking Guides Ltd

Photographs
All photographs in this book were taken by the
authors, Ros & David Brawn

Front Cover Photographs

16th Century Gate
&Belfry,
Aracena Castle

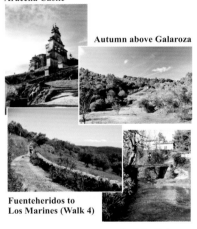

Autumn above Galaroza

Fuenteheridos to
Los Marines (Walk 4)

Castaño-Galaroza
(Walk 19)

Sierra de Aracena
- a Walk! Guidebook

CONTENTS

David & Ros Brawn

David and Ros have lived and worked in England, Papua New Guinea and the Seychelles before settling for a number of years in Tenerife. David's first published books were accountancy texts.

David and Ros have been walking and writing for Discovery Walking Guides since it began, researching guides for most of the Canary Islands, the Balearic Islands, Malta, Gozo, Madeira, the Alpujarras and the Sierra de Aracena. More recently they have surveyed and mapped a number of these regions using satellite navigation equipment combined with cartographic software.

Considering themselves as semi-permanent travellers, they divide their non-research time between Spain and Northampton, England.

David is a member of the British Cartographic Society.

David & Ros are the authors of a number of publications to various destinations including:

Tour & Trail Maps
Tour & Trail Super-Durable Maps
Walkers' Maps
Drive! Maps
34/35 Walks Guidebooks
Walk! Guidebooks

David is also the author of:

GPS The Easy Way

FIRST IMPRESSIONS

The high ridges of the **Sierra de Aracena** lie in the north of Spain's Huelva province, almost rubbing shoulders with the Portuguese border. If you approach it from the south, you'll notice the subtle changes in the landscape, harder lines and colours giving way to rolling emerald pastures frequently dotted with olive, chestnut and oak, or providing pasture for tranquil cows or sheep. The higher *sierras* form a misty backdrop, and now the hills and valleys become more rugged as you travel deeper into the region, the trees more ancient and twisted, often providing shade and acorns for the black Iberian pigs that are so important to the region's economy. Thinly scattered *pueblos* and small towns sit on rises or lie tucked into folded valleys. There's a feeling of having passed through a time warp, and if you spend a few days here exploring the towns, villages and countryside, you'll find yourself adapting to the relaxed pace of life.

THE TOWN OF ARACENA

Castle ruins and the **Iglesia Prioral de Nuestra Señora del Mayor Dolor** (13-14th century) dominate the main town of the region (pop. 7000), worth a visit in their own right and for the excellent panoramic views from this high point. If you are interested in religious architecture you'll find plenty to please spanning several centuries, and there are many other buildings of interest, not least the splendidly ornate **Casino de Arias Montano** which can be contemplated from the terrace tables of **Bar Manzano** in the **Plaza Marqués de Aracena**. Streets radiate from the *plaza* where a few quirky shops sell anything from hams to hunting equipment or good value footwear. There's even an **internet café**, and if you need anything photocopying then go to the jeweller's near **Bar Manzano**.

The belltower entrance to Aracena Castle

There are two information points we recommend visiting, particularly the **Centro de Interpretación del Parque/Visitors' Centre** (10.00-14.00 & 16.00-18.00) which is housed in the impressive **Cabildo Viejo** (old town hall, 15th century), and the **Tourist Information Office** (10.00-13.30 & 15.00-18.00) near the entrance to the **Gruta de las Maravillas**, where you'll also find the **Museo Geológico Minero** (free entry, hours as for the Tourist Information Office).

The most visited place in the town is the **Gruta de Las Maravillas** or Cave of Marvels, (10.00-13.30 & 15.00-18.00, €7 adults, €5 children), over two kilometres of caves and lakes underneath the hill on which the **Castillo de**

Aracena stands. First mentioned in historic documents in 1886, they were drained and first opened to the public in 1914, soon becoming a famous tourist attraction for the Spanish. About one kilometre is visited on guided tours, the inter-linked caves filled with stalactites and stalagmites, each 'room' whimsically named; for example, 'The Room of the Nudes' and 'Crystals of the Gods'. Take a jacket - it's cold underground. In the areas around the *grutas*, and in other public areas of the town, you'll come across various pieces of contemporary sculpture, described as an open air museum - unfortunately, some pieces have attracted the attention of another kind of modern artist, the graffiti specialist.

ALÁJAR

At around 1000 inhabitants, this ranks as a significant *pueblo*, though more people probably view it from the heights of **Peña de Arias Montano** than visit its marble-cobbled streets. The hill itself offers views over **Alájar** and beyond, and boasts a waterfall, café and restaurant, and the **Ermita de Nuestra Señora de los Angeles**. Artefacts and local produce are sometimes on sale (we once saw a dog serving on one of the stalls), but the toilet facilities are not recommended. (You can reach the hill by car or on foot, but if you want to reach the very top, follow Walk 15.)

Alájar's *plaza*

Alájar itself (Arabic for 'stone') is a serene, neat place, the hub of which is its attractively cobbled central **Plaza d'España** bordered by white two storey buildings, some with balconies, or decorated with tiles and with wrought iron work protecting their windows. The interior of **Restaurante Mesón El Corcho** ('House of Cork', in the square) is both a feast for the eyes and a recommended eating experience - not the cheapest place in the region, but unforgettable. We dashed in soaked to the skin during a thunderstorm after walking for a couple of tough hours and the staff, not put out by our dishevelled appearance, served us with style and good food, but first shovelled a pan of hot embers from the open fire to place under our table to warm us. They have a bar fronting the square if you don't want to eat, but do try to at least sneak a look in the restaurant (a former theatre) behind it. (Walks 9, 10 & 11)

ALMONASTER LA REAL

The land around this settlement (pop. 2500) supports a variety of crops and livestock; at one time there were mines here producing copper, zinc and manganese. Unsurprisingly then, the area has been settled by various groups since pre-Roman times, and there's even an Islamic Cultural Festival held in October to raise awareness of the area's history and to foster understanding between religions. The main streets are lined with fragrant orange trees, and a stroll between the neat white houses is recommended, though the eye is always drawn to the 10th century mosque the **Mezquita**, built on the hill overlooking the main part of the town. Climb up to enjoy both the beautifully preserved building and the views, and ascend the watchtower if you want to look down into the 19th century bullring built beside it. Within the little town itself are various buildings of note, including the 18th century **Ermita de la Trinidad** with its triple bell tower in **Plaza de la Ayuntamiento**, and the precarious-looking **Iglesia de San Martín** with nesting storks on its tower in spring and early summer.

The *mezquita* at Almonaster la Real

When you're in need of a refreshment stop, try the large, cool terrace of **Hotel Casa García** just off the main road running past the north of the town, or the bar in **Plaza de la Ayuntamiento** where you can also try your luck at the Spanish version of the lottery or football pools while taking refreshments. (Walk 24)

CASTAÑO DEL ROBLEDO

The river **Río Múrgia** rises in this tranquil village of about 250 inhabitants, established in 1554. Many of the houses and buildings are Renaissance and Baroque in style, built between the 15th and 18th centuries, and there is a timeless quality to the pale cobbled streets, their buildings seemingly little changed over the generations. The village has two churches, one unfinished; the other is the **Iglesia de Santiago Apóstol**. (Walks 12, 16 & 19)

CORTEGANA

The Roman-Gothic style 14th Century **Castillo de Cortegana** stands out on the skyline as you approach this rather tired town (pop. 2000), one of those places that looks better from a distance. The preserved atmosphere that pervades many of the region's other centres of population is largely absent in the town, although the peak on which the castle sits is worth a visit. An information board outside the church and its *ermita* details the construction of the castle, and explains its importance in the front line of defence against the Portuguese who disputed the ownership of this part of Spain.

Within the town is a 16th century church, the **Iglesia Parroquial de San Salvador** which has been declared a National Monument; built on a larger scale than usual at 31 by 20 metres. Perhaps the town's greatest importance to the visitor is that the only supermarket of reasonable size in the region is located here. (Walk 26 & 27)

FUENTEHERIDOS

The well-preserved marble-cobbled streets and traditional buildings of this 13th century village (pop. 700) have earned it the status of 'Conjunto Histórico-Artístico' (place of historic/artistic interest) awarded by the Spanish authorities in 1982.

Fuente de los Doce Caños

This fertile area is blessed with abundant water, as the two million litres of water gushing ceaselessly from the **Fuente de los Doce Caños** in the main square illustrates. The people of this village were the first to grow potatoes brought from America, and are therefore known as *Paperos*. Stroll around the narrow, sometimes steep streets to appreciate the architecture and flower-hung balconies, and take a look at the 18th century Baroque **Iglesia Parroquial del Espíritu Santo**.

The square also offers a choice of restaurants and bars; our recommendation is the welcoming **Bar Diablo**. The food is fairly basic (as is the furniture), but everything is fresh and tasty. It's the meeting place of choice for the locals and almost always lively. (Walks 4, 21 & 22)

GALAROZA

The tranquility of this little town of about 1700 inhabitants belies its turbulent history of earthquakes in the 18th century and the looting of its treasures in 1810-11. This fertile and well-irrigated area produces apples, peaches, cherries and chestnuts, and locally made handicrafts of wood and basketwork are on sale. There are a number of buildings of note, including the stone-built 16th century **Iglesia Parroquial de la Purísima Concepción**, restored after the earthquake of 1755. There are a few bar/restaurants, including **Bar Venecia** on the main road to Portugal. (Walks 17 & 19)

LINARES DE LA SIERRA

Marble 'doormats'

Marble cobbled mosaic 'door mats' decorate the entrances of many of the village houses, several of which are enhanced by wrought iron balconies and pots of bright flowers.(Walks 5, 6, 7, 8, 9 & 10) Now reduced to about 350 inhabitants, the village saw better days when the production of olive oil and grinding of grain were important at the start of the 20th century.

Of note is the **Plaza de Toros de Linares de la Sierra** sitting below the rather neglected church *plaza*. The bullring also does service as an unofficial car park, a ceramic wall plaque recording its 'decommissioning' in 1992 as a venue for the genuine killing of bulls, although mock fights with young animals who are not harmed take place on some *fiestas*. There's a very rustic bar opening out onto the sand floor of the ring, recommended for its location rather than its catering or service.

If anywhere in the region can be called industrial, then this town of 2,500 is it. Its name is synonymous with the best hams in Spain, and trade appears to be thriving, judging by the large, businesslike industrial units that process the Iberian pig into hams, pork products and sausages of every type. Ancient records prove that the town provided hams for Spanish royalty from the 15th century, and a stroll through its streets soon underlines the importance of the trade today; almost every business seems connected to the pig, and in summer the air hangs heavy with the aroma of ham. If you are vegetarian, then we'd suggest you eat elsewhere. (Walks 17)

CORTELAZOR

This little town of around 450 inhabitants has the dubious honour of recording the highest annual rainfall in the province of Huelva, though this has assisted in the production of olive oil, grapes for wine making, fruits, vegetables and the rearing of pigs. The rebel Moslem leader Azor seized the town; hence, the 'Court of Azor'.

The **Iglesia de San Juan Bautista** houses some worthy religious sculptures and a painting by Alonso de Tovar, who studied under Murillo.

Cortelazor

The grey and white marble cobbles and white houses with wrought iron, flower-decked balconies are typical of the region, and there are a couple of handily located bars in the main square. (Walks 22 & 23)

SANTA ANA LA REAL

Several villages in the region are enjoying a new lease of life, as Spanish city dwellers escape for a break to the countryside, sometimes to their second homes. This is one such village, experiencing a rebirth after the traditional pursuits of farming were gradually abandoned, leading to depopulation. Now the population stands at around 650 inhabitants. This is an attractive area surrounded by chestnut and acorn woods, and even the growing of fruits and vegetables are gaining importance once again. (Walks 12 & 13)

Ceramic plaque in Santa Ana

Coreterrangel's church

This sleepy hamlet seems to be populated by cats, dogs and a few black-clad, amicable old ladies. Unusual in that its church is situated in a field a couple of hundred metres away from the village, its *plaza* has a washing trough, a couple of benches, some *Cercis siliquastrum* trees and a drinking water tap but, unfortunately, no bar. (Walk 23)

LOS MADROÑEROS

If you want to see a village as it really looked before the motor vehicle made everywhere accessible, then this is the one. A narrow dirt lane exists for the determined driver, but the best access is on foot (see Walks 9 & 14). This *pueblo* was completely abandoned for years, but recently people have been drifting in to make the ancient cottages habitable again, if only for weekend hideaways, made easier by the supply of water that still flows from its *fuente*, and also by modern technology such as solar collectors and mobile phones.

Los Madroñeros

The tiny centre of the village resembles a Medieval settlement, and it still has its own church. It's probably one of those 'see it now before it changes' places.

Although there has been a gradual depopulation of many towns and villages, the equable climate, pure air, abundance of water and willingness to carry out labour-intensive working methods has ensured the continuation of traditional trades, if on a modest scale. Now that tourism is beginning to have a positive effect on the region's economy, these traditional pursuits are gaining in importance.

One aspect of the local economy that has remained strong for many generations is the Iberian ham industry. The *Pata Negra* ham from this region is a highly prized delicacy across Spain and beyond, thanks to an ideal combination of climate, rich soil, acorn-bearing Holm oaks and black Iberian pigs. The town of **Jabugo** is the home of the largest

Iberian pigs

ham producing businesses, but the influences of this vital economic activity makes itself felt in the entire region. You'll see these acorn-fed pigs across the *sierras*, and most hostelries will serve a bewildering variety of pork based dishes.

A cork factory outside Aracena

As well as producing acorns, the thick bark of the Cork Oak (Quercus suber) is collected and used to manufacture wine corks, cork matting and tiles.

Cork oaks near Alájar

Mature trees are 'barked' every nine years using sharp knives, those most recently harvested bearing a broad deep red-brown scar around the trunk.

Autumn is peak time for *setas*, or wild mushrooms and fungi. This region has hundreds of species, and many Aracenans are experts on them - just as well as there are plenty of toxic varieties. Those that are good to eat come in all shapes, sizes and colours, and most of these feature in recipes unique to the region on bar and restaurant menus across the region during the main season, around October to November.

Setas

Spanish visitors come from far and wide to sample these unique delicacies. If you are here in November, look out for the *setas* festival held in **Aracena**. And do try at least one local dish; *setas revueltos* (scrambled eggs with wild mushrooms) is simple yet popular.

Sloping, irregular fields of pollarded chestnut trees (Castanea sativa) undulate across much of the area. Mostly ancient, gnarled and twisted into fairytale shapes, the trees produce their crops of nuts in October and November, when they are harvested in time-honoured fashion. The villagers - usually women - gather in groups for the *apaño*; the collection of fallen nuts, sometimes beating the trees with sticks to encourage their fall.

Pollarded chestnut trees

Cattle, sheep, horses and goats are also important to the economy. If you are here in May you might catch the *Feria de Ganados* held in **Aracena** where farmers show their best animals and compete for awards, as well as enjoying a three-day festival of gossip, drinking and eating. A wide range of vegetables, fruits and nuts is grown, including potatoes, tomatoes, salad vegetables, root crops, citrus fruits, olives, peaches and cherries, as well as grapes destined for wine making, though most are produced on a small scale.

Most of the once thriving copper mines are closed now, though the quarrying of marble still continues, but on a reduced scale. Metalwork craftsmen are now more likely to make items for the tourist trade, although the wrought metalwork around the windows in many of the towns and villages was produced locally by previous generations of craftsmen.

'HERD' DOGS OF THE SIERRAS

Farm dogs, barking either to guard their territory or simply at something different happening in their simple lives, are common to many of the destinations for which we research our walking guides. When walking in the Sierra de Aracena it is easy to dismiss all barking dogs in a similar manner and miss one of the remarkable features of the region; 'herd' dogs.

In the Sierras, livestock is housed overnight in *cortijos* and then released each morning to graze the abundant pasture, returning at night to the *cortijo*. Normally you would expect to find the flocks and herds escorted by a farm worker but in this region they use dogs. Not just any dogs, but specially trained 'herd' dogs who guide the livestock out to the pasture and bring it back at night. During the day the dogs guard the herd/flock against threats, in the old days from wolves and lynx cats and in more recent times from rustlers. Usually the dogs work in pairs, setting up a warning barking as we approach and possibly shepherding the herd/flock away.

We've encountered 'herd' dogs alongside a number of our walking routes, always the other side of a stone wall or fence. Unlike English sheep dogs, there is no common breed used as 'herd' dogs, as they range from small terriers up to Pyrenean Mountain dogs. Always remember that these are working dogs protecting their herd/flock, so never try to pet them while they are at work; get too close and seem to be threatening their charges and they may attack. Simply walk past and as you distance yourself the aggressive barking will subside as the 'herd' dogs resume their pastoral watchfulness.

Off duty, and off their property, 'herd' dogs are no longer aggressive. In our encounter on Walk 4 (Wp.9) two thirty kilo herd dogs decided we were to be befriended before their working day started, and on Walk 19 an off duty 'herd' dog accompanied us most of the way to **Galaroza**.

BRAND LOYALTY

While walking in the Sierra de Aracena we pass many impressive entrance gates to country properties, most appearing to simply guard an area of common pasture. Some of these entrances boast the property's name, and nearly all carry a hieroglyphic design. These designs are the 'brand' used to identify livestock belonging to the property.

The branding of livestock enables ranchers to identify strays and return them to their rightful owner, but principally is a discouragement to rustlers. Branded livestock is identified with the rancher and a stranger/rustler trying to sell stolen stock would immediately attract attention. Few ranchers live on their property, preferring the modern comforts of electricity and running water of life in town and commuting to their herds each day. For these relatively unsupervised properties, livestock branding provides some degree of security.

While pondering the many brands and 'herd' dogs of the Sierra de Aracena, we were disappointed not to come across a property named 'The Ponderosa', but even without this, the brands and 'herd' dogs identify this region as Spain's 'Wild West'.

WHEN TO GO, WHERE TO STAY

CLIMATE

There's a good reason why the Sierra de Aracena is lush and green. It has plenty of rainfall, and most of it falls in late autumn and winter. The nights turn cold and can reach 3°C, and you'll need warm waterproof clothing and a liking for getting wet and muddy if you walk in these seasons. The summer months of July and August are hot (to 30°C), but if you are determined to walk here in summer, then choose shady, woodland routes only, and go well prepared with sun protection and lots of drinking water. But if you want to get the best out of your visit, then choose autumn or spring.

Autumn gives you the advantage of experiencing show-stopping colours, as the chestnut groves turn to flaming gold and russet. The harvests of chestnuts, walnuts, almonds and apples are gathered and this is the time when those locals who know the difference between the tasty and the toxic collect bewildering varieties of *setas*, served up in almost every bar and restaurant according to unique recipes.

By spring, the land is heavy with moisture, and you'll probably get your feet wet on most walks. But the best of the spring flowers bloom from late March to the end of May, and the days are steadily lengthening. If you want to see some of the best natural flower meadows and plant-stuffed paths on the planet, then it has to be in spring.

ACCOMMODATION

As public transport is scanty at best, and taxis are hard to find, we assume that you'll have the use of a car - in this case, the location of your accommodation is flexible. At the time of research, we saw billboards proudly announcing a big new hotel due to open near **Aracena**, but as we haven't seen any sign of it, we will stick with what we know is available. Full details of accommodation can be found at the back of this book, including some of the *casas rurales* that are dotted around the region in Appendices, P.129. There are a couple of campsites offering good facilities (see Appendices).

Alájar This is an elegant little town, handy for walking routes and with a couple of good restaurants. There's a one star *posada* right in town. **Almonaster la Real** Probably the most historically interesting and well preserved of the towns, there's one largish two star hotel and a couple of one star establishments. Well placed for access to walks. **Aracena** There are obvious advantages to staying here; you have a reasonable choice of shops, bars and restaurants, there's a handful of walks starting (and sometimes finishing) from the town, and if you are desperate to pick up your email, the only internet café in the region is here. There are two hotels and a pension near the centre of town. **Corteconcepción** Don't expect much nightlife in this sleepy setting, but there are two hostel-restaurants in this little town. **Cortegana** There's a pension in town, though we wouldn't especially recommend **Cortegana** as a base. **Fuenteheridos** As well as the pension in town, there is a three star rural hotel just a kilometre down the road. There are a few reasonably well stocked food shops, well patronised bars and restaurants, and a pleasant convivial atmosphere in the 'main' square. **Galaroza** You have a choice of a two star hotel, a hostel and a pension. The town is pleasant and is well located for walking routes. **Jabugo** There is a four star hotel and a pension in this ham town, but you've got to like being surrounded by the ham trade and its scents at all times. **Los Marines** There's a *finca* with accommodation just outside this little village, but you won't be able to stroll out to an evening hostelry for a drink from here. **Santa Ana la Real** Standing on its own just outside **Santa Ana** is a fairly basic hostel/restaurant.

Bear in mind that, if you stay in one of the out-of-town *fincas* or *casas rurales*, you are likely to be some distance (on foot) from sampling the nightlife delights of the region. Although these don't amount to more than restaurants and bars, this might be important in planning your accommodation. Or you could split you stay between a couple of places.

If you are staying in a *casa rural* or on one of the campsites, and are thinking of self-catering, be aware that there are few large supermarkets, although all but the smallest villages have a little shop for basic goods. The nearest thing to a Tescos is in **Cortegana**.

FLORA & FAUNA

Autumn above Galaroza

Plenty of rain, warm summers, rolling countryside peppered with chestnut woods and oak forests, and a lack of pollution work together to provide the ideal habitat for many species of flora and fauna. Here, we only have space to mention a few of them.

Cistus ladanifer

Ancient forests of chestnuts (Castanea sativa), often pollarded, and several types of oak including the cork oak (Quercus suber) and holm oak (Quercus rotundifolia) whose sweet acorns form the staple diet for the herds of pigs, are the most numerous trees in the *sierra*. There are plenty of other species, such as the olive (Olea europaea), white poplar (Populus alba), alder (Alnus glutinosa), maritime pine (Pinus pinaster) and umbrella pine (Pinus pinea), and the nettle tree (Celtis australis).

Borago officinalis

Away from the denser areas of trees, small trees and shrubs of various species thrive. We saw several varieties of rockrose, or cistus, including the flamboyant gum cistus (Cistus ladanifer) with flowers to 9cm across. Commonly found are yellow broom (Genista scorpius), rosemary (Rosmarinus officinalis), tree heather (Erica scoparia), the strawberry tree (Arbutus unedo), laurustinus (Viburnum tinus) and the mastic tree

(Pistacia lentiscus). Fruit and nut trees of many types thrive around the towns and villages and citrus trees are used to line streets, for their scent and ornamental value.

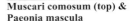

When it comes to wild flowers, the task of attempting to give an overview of varieties must be left to an expert with far more space than we have here. Orchids, peonies, lavenders - suffice it to say, that we were amazed at the abundance and variety of flowers, particularly in spring, and that there were plenty we hadn't seen before. And the varieties of wild mushroom, the *setas*, are almost as numerous.

**Muscari comosum (top) &
Paeonia mascula**

We hoped we might see an Iberian lynx (Lynx pardina) or mountain cat (Felis catus), both common to the area, but they are quick to detect the noise of walkers approaching. We were rewarded, though, by a face-to-face encounter with an otter (Lutra lutra), and if you are lucky you could see badgers (Meles meles) and deer.

Horses in an Alájar field

Farm animals include, of course, the famous pigs as well as sheep, goats and cattle and there are plenty of horses. We saw imperial eagles (Aguila chrysaetos) and black vultures (Aegypius monachus), and there are plenty more birds of prey for the expert to look out for including several other types of eagle, and goshawks (Accipiter gentilis). Herons (Ardea cinerea) are common, colonies of them nesting in high trees, and kingfishers (Alcedo atthis) can be spotted near the reservoirs.

Easy even for the amateur to spot are the common storks which nest on church spires in the spring and early summer and there are the rarer black storks (Ciconia negra) which might be spotted near water. There are too many other bird species to mention here, but you should see (or at least, hear) some of them while walking.

A stork on its huge nest

Lizards and snakes, including the common viper, are numerous, and the streams and rivers are home to salamander, fresh water tortoises and eels as well as abundant fish and insect life.

Our brief summary is intended only as a 'taster', as space is limited.

Almonaster's 19th century bullring

The Sierra de Aracena has a long history, reflected in its architecture. You will find village houses little changed since they were built half a millennium or more ago, while churches, religious buildings and *ermitas* spanning eight hundred years are still in regular use. The

Iglesia de San Martín, Almonaster la Real

influence of the Arabs as far back as the third century is still obvious from their systems of public water supplies, still in use in some villages.

To get a feel for the long history of the region, stroll around the town of **Almonaster la Real** and visit the hilltop mosque (10th century, photo P.9), built on the site of a Roman castle, with the bullring sharing this elevated position. Almost every building in this small town is steeped in historical significance, including the **Iglesia de San Martín** (14th century), an alarmingly frail-looking edifice topped with nesting storks.

Almonaster la Real is not alone in possessing a long history. Most of the towns and villages in the region have been settled for many generations. The region's main town of **Aracena** boasts many significant historic buildings, not least the Arab castle (13-14th centuries), and the fifteenth century **Cabildo**

Aracena's Plaza del Marqués de Aracena

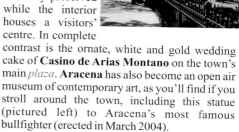

Viejo, (photo P.25) its exterior carefully preserved while the interior houses a visitors' centre. In complete contrast is the ornate, white and gold wedding cake of **Casino de Arias Montano** on the town's main *plaza*. **Aracena** has also become an open air museum of contemporary art, as you'll find if you stroll around the town, including this statue (pictured left) to Aracena's most famous bullfighter (erected in March 2004).

Jabugo's statue to the ham workers

Other towns are now following suit, erecting modern works of art in public areas such as this statue to workers in the *jamón serrano* industry in **Jabugo** which doubles as a modern *fuente*.

Religious architecture is found in almost every settlement, often embellished with ceramic plaques honouring their patron saints, and ceramic tile mosaics decorate church spires, some buildings of importance, and public *fuentes*, such as the once elegant **Santa Ana** example, now in urgent need of refurbishment.

Take a look inside the **Ermita de Nuestra Señora de Los Ángeles** on the **Peña de Arias Montana**, its ornate interior contrasting with the understated exterior.

Santa Ana's *fuente*

Visit **Los Madroñeros** to see village cottages at their most typical and basic. (photo P.12) Homes in larger villages and towns may be two storeys high, sometimes more, often with wrought iron window bars and narrow balconies dripping with flowers. (photo P.11)

Many streets are paved with white marble cobbles or mosaics of white and pale grey, particularly notable in **Linares de la Sierra**. (photo P.10)

Ceramic plaque in Alájar

Ermita de Nuestra Señora de los Ángeles

Because there is little evidence of replacing the old with the new, almost every settlement and town in the region is a living history lesson, a rich heritage still intact.

The cuisine of the Sierra de Aracena is closely based upon pork in all its guises, along with seasonal vegetables, fruits, nuts, vegetables and a unique range of *setas* (mushrooms and edible fungi). We found the quality and freshness of food served in bars and restaurants from humble to posh to be very good almost everywhere, and the usual advice to travellers of. "Eat where the locals eat." certainly works for this region. Most of the local recipes are simple, but if you are working with fresh, local produce, much of it organic, you can't go far wrong.

One little problem you might encounter is understanding the menu (or *carta*). A few places used to foreign visitors might have an English translation, but many *típicos* have a chalk board as their menu which probably changes daily. Even more minimalist are places such as Swifty's (see P.134) where there is no written menu at all. You simply sit down while the boss or young waiter reels off a list of the day's choices for starter and main course.

Breakfast (*desayuno*)
Not a big deal here, even in the more expensive hotels, so don't expect the full English even though there is an abundance of pork. The locals have *tostados*, thick, chunky toast with one of several toppings including *unto* (lard), *manteca colorá* (coloured butter) with thin slices of *lomo* (pork), *aceite de oliva y ajo* (olive oil and garlic), olive oil with *jamón serrano de pata negra* (the famous cured ham of Sierra de Aracena), *miel* (honey) or *mermeledas* (fruit jams). Croissants and chocolate-filled *churros*, a soft sweet pastry, might be offered. Coffee is the most usual breakfast drink, often with *leche* (milk) although later in the day other versions of coffee are more popular (see **drinks**, below).

Lunch (*merienda*)
Bars and restaurants catering for working people often offer a *menú del día*, a low priced two or three course meal with bread and a beer or soft drink. There's usually a choice of three or four dishes for each course, served swiftly. Usual times for lunch are about 13.00 - 15.00. There's often a choice of *sopa* (soup) or *gazpacho* (cold tomato based soup), salad or pasta for starters, or *revueltos de setas* (when in season) or *de espinacas* (scrambled eggs with mushrooms or with spinach). Main courses might offer *pechuga de pollo* (chicken breast), *chuleta de cerdo* (pork chop) or *filete de pescado* (fish fillet) served with a few (real, home made) chips or potatoes and small salad or roasted peppers. Desserts are simple. Usually there's *natillas* or *flan de la casa*, both of which are little more complicated than custard with a dusting of cinnamon, or a choice of *frutas* (fresh fruit) or *helados* (ice cream).

Dinner (*comida*)
Most Spanish people consider the evening meal to be the main meal of the day, and as it doesn't usually begin much before nine or ten at night, this could just be too late for flagging walkers.

There might be a soup starter, or a plate of mixed titbits of different types of ham, pork and cheese. Stews are also popular, known in this region as *guisos*, which might contain potatoes, pork ribs or liver. If you see the local equivalent of Shark's Fin Soup on the menu, *guiso de orejas*, (stewed ears) take care not to confuse this delicacy with the similarly named dessert of *guiso de orejones*, a less startling offering of sun-dried peaches in syrup or liqueur.

Meat courses are dominated, of course, by pork served in a hundred ways, though there might be a choice of *pollo* (chicken), *ternera* (veal), *chivo* or *cabra (*goat), *cola de toro (*oxtail) or fillet steak. Main courses are often served with just a garnish of vegetables, though the Spanish often order an *ensalada* (salad) to eat either before or along with the main course. Although fish might be on the menu, you are unlikely to find a wide choice, though the *trucha* (trout) from local streams and rivers is very good. You'll find plenty more unique dishes on offer when *setas* are available, best in October-November.

Desserts are often fruit or nut based, drawing on local supplies of almonds, chestnuts, apples, pears, citrus fruits, peaches, and so on. *Queso fresco de cabra con miel* is a delicious slice of soft white goat's cheese served with honey and sometimes a few nuts or dried fruits. And there's always ice cream or *natillas*.

Snacks
If you want an informal meal then head for a bar with a servery of tasty treats displayed behind glass. Some places have a hot servery and a cold one. Order small portions or *tapas* if you want a taste of several different snacks, or ask for *raciones* if you want a larger serving. You might have a choice of twenty or thirty snacks, and you can choose by pointing at the ones you want. If you want a sandwich, ask for a *bocadillo* although the bread used for these is often disappointing.

Drinks
Many bars in the region still maintain the tradition of free *tapas* when you order a drink. Little plates of anything from olives, shavings of *jamón*, *queso*, (cheese), nuts or pickled kidney beans (*habichuelas*) might be served.

Non-alcoholic beverages include coffee in various versions, from *cortado*, a small glass of strong black coffee with a splash of milk on top, *café solo* (a small black coffee), *café con leche* (a milky coffee served in a cup or tall glass). Tea is available (*té*) in bars, but is usually supplied as a cup of hot water with tea bag on the side: you might need to ask for milk (*leche*). Familiar brands of soft drinks (*refrescos*) are readily available, as are *agua sin* or *con gas* (still or fizzy water). If you want pure squeezed orange juice, look for a hostelry with a machine full of oranges behind the bar, and ask for *zumo de naranja* .

There's a wide choice of alcoholic drinks in most bars and restaurants, including *cerveza* (lager style beer) in bottles, cans or *presión* (draught). Ask for a *vino blanco* and you'll be served a dry sherry type of drink, or ask for *tinto* (red) or the not so easy to find *rosado* (rosé). There's every kind of spirit you can think of and more prominently displayed behind most bars - but beware of the very generous measures. If you don't want to pay the price of a brand such as Smirnoff or Gordon's then ask for a *nacional*, a Spanish brand equivalent.

a la plancha	grilled
a la romana	battered
aceite de oliva	olive oil
aceitunas	olives
agua (sin gas, natural)	water (plain)
agua con gaz	fizzy water
aguacate	avocado
ajo	garlic
al horno	oven cooked
albaricoques	apricots
albóndigas	meatballs
alioli	garlic mayonnaise
almendras	almonds
angulas	elvers (young eels)
arroz	rice
asado	roast
atún	tuna
azúcar	sugar
bacalao	cod
berenjenas	aubergine
bocadillo	sandwich, roll
bofes	sweetbreads
cabra	goat
cacahuetes	peanuts
café	coffee
calamares	squid
carne	meat
castañas	chestnuts
cazuela	stew
cebollas	onions
cerdo	pork
cerezas	cherries
cerveza	lager type beer
chivito	kid
chivo	goat
chorizo	spicy pork sausage
chuleta	chop
cola de toro	bull's tail (oxtail)
comida	food, main meal
conejo	rabbit
cordero	lamb
desayuno	breakfast
embutido	sausage
ensalada	salad
espinacas	spinach
faisán	pheasant
flan	creme caramel
fresas	strawberries
fritas	chips
frito	fried
fruta	fruit
gambas	prawns
garbanzos	chickpeas
gazpacho	cold tomato based vegetable soup
guisantes	peas
guiso de orejas	stewed ears (of pig)
guiso de orejones	sun-dried peaches in syrup
helados	icecream
higos	figs
huevos	eggs
jamón	ham
judias	beans
leche	milk
lechuga	lettuce
lentejas	lentils
limón	lemon
lomo	loin of pork
mantequilla	butter
manzana	apple
mariscos	seafood
mejillones	mussels
merienda	lunch
merluza	hake
mero	grouper
miel	honey
mollejas	sweetbreads
morcilla	black pudding
naranja	orange
nata	cream
natillas	custard
nueces	walnuts
olla serrana	meat & veg stew
pan	bread
papas	potatoes
pasas	raisins
pato	duck
pavo	turkey
pescado	fish
plátanos	bananas
pollo	chicken
pulpo	octopus
queso	cheese
rape	monkfish
refresco	sweet fizzy drink
revueltos	scrambled eggs
salchicha	sausage
salchichón	salami type sausage
salmón	salmon
salsa	sauce
setas	wild mushrooms
solomillo	pork loin
sopa de cazador	game soup
tapas	small dish of food
té	tea
ternera	veal
tomate	tomato
trucha	trout
turrón	nougat-like sweet
uvas	grapes
verduras	vegetables
vino (tinto, rosado, blanco)	wine (red, rosé, white
zanahorias	carrots

THINGS TO DO (other than walking)

RÍO TINTO (Red River) MINES

Not just mines, this is a region shaped by 5000 years of mining. Minerals tint the earth, rivers and streams, not only red, but blue, green and orange. Go south from **Aracena** on the A 479 to **Campofrío**, then onto the A461 to the **Minas de Río Tinto**, an entire town dedicated to mining, and now to tourists visiting its heritage. Visit the Mining Museum first, to get an impression of the scale, both in size and generations, of this area rich in copper, sulphur, silver and gold. Commercial mining began here in Roman times, and there's a claustrophobic 'Roman Mine' you can visit within the museum. The British influence from the 19th century is well covered; don't miss the artefacts and photos in Rooms 11 & 12, and Room 14 with the Maharajah's Carriage (1892) which was built for Queen Victoria's (cancelled) trip to India.

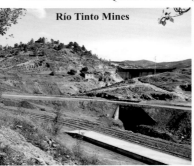
Río Tinto Mines

Unlikely as it might seem, the English brought football to Spain. In 1873 some English expatriates working for **Río Tinto** kicked a ball around and introduced some of their Spanish workmates to the beautiful game This is now acknowledged by the Spanish as the beginnings of the sport in their country in the 'Birth of Football' monument erected in 2003.

Book your train ride through the huge mines themselves while in the museum. Also worth seeing in the town itself is the **Barrio de Bella Vista**, a 'little England' colony built for the company workers. There's a link with the town of **Aracena** too, where the spacious houses built at **Aracenilla** by the mining company so that their executives could have weekends away, still stand.

EMBALSE DE ARACENA

Embalse de Aracena

A few kilometres north-east of the town of **Aracena** lies the **Embalse de Aracena** which, in addition to storing water, provides a haven for wildlife (particularly birds) and recreation for humans. Although we've yet to find its café open, there are picnic areas, and swimming and fishing is permitted. When we last visited, the public areas looked rather tired and could have done with some tidying up, but even so it's a serene and restful area. Leave **Aracena** on the HV 3116 which passes through **Carboneras** on its way to the reservoir.

Aracena's Cabildo Viejo

Confusingly it's sometimes wrongly referred to as the Tourist Information Office (which is the one near the Cave of Marvels), perhaps forgiveable as its full name of **Centro De Visitantes de la Sierra de Aracena y Picos de Aroche, Reserva de la Biosfera de las Dehesas de Sierra Morena** is a bit of a mouthful. It is housed in the **Cabildo Viejo**, the elegant old 15th century town hall **in Plaza Alta** in **Aracena**. Its purpose is to inform about the natural environment of the area and is dedicated to the conservation and protection of the environment. There's usually a pleasant receptionist, but only Spanish is spoken. Entry to the exhibition is free, and it's well worth spending time here to gain a greater understanding of the region. Open from 10.00 - 14.00 & 16.00 - 18.00.

LA GRUTA DE LAS MARAVILLAS

Entrance to La Gruta

This attraction draws coachloads of Spanish visitors to **Aracena** at weekends and on fiestas, so to save queuing choose another time (between 10.00 to 13.30 and 15.00 to 18.00, every day, €7). Open to the public since 1914, guides will take you on an hour's walk through more than a kilometre of whimsically-named caverns and lakes, weird rock colourations and formations. (See additional notes in First Impressions, Towns & Villages). There's also a small mining and mineral museum and tourist information office near the cave entrance.

Also…

If your accommodation has no pool you can swim at the **Piscina Municipal** in **Aracena**, or in the **Embalse de Aracena** (see above). Most horse riding comes as part of a package along with accommodation, but you can hire by the day from **Picadero La Suerte** or from **Finca El Moro**, (please phone Finca El Moro first) (details in Appendices). Go up to **Peña de Arias Montano** (see also notes in Introduction) even if you aren't doing Walk 15, a wonderful look out point with 16th century *ermita* and belfry, if made a bit tacky by the cheap pottery and gewgaws sometimes sold by gloomy stallholders. To find out about the pork industry, go to the **Museo del Jamón** in **Plaza de Doña Elvira**, **Aracena**, or visit the **Cinco Jotas** ham factory in **Jabugo** (see Appendices), though you'll probably be talked into buying some produce at the end of your tour. There's a tourist 'train' ride of about one hour which leaves from the **Plaza de San Pedro** near the entrance to the caves in **Aracena** though booking is done in the **Cabildo Viejo** (see above) there's a town route for €4 and a longer trip taking in a wider area for €10.

The **Sierra de Aracena** is part of the most westerly province of the Spanish Autonomous Community of **Andalucía**, itself the Iberian Peninsula's most southerly territory, just 15 kilometres across the sea from Africa. The territory comprises **Huelva**, **Cádiz**, **Sevilla**, **Córdoba**, **Málaga**, **Granada**, **Jaén** and **Almería**. The influences that formed **Andalucía** came from successions of invaders over many centuries. Some of the deepest and most lasting influences result from seven hundred years of Moorish occupation; even the name of the province has barely changed from the Moorish 'al-Andalus'.

The Phoenicians, traders from modern day Lebanon, were the first recorded colonists in Andalucía, establishing several ports including **Cádiz** (Europe's oldest city) around 1100 BC. Trading links were established, towns and villages sprang up and farming, mining and fishing became important industries. Others saw the potential of the area and moved in, including Greeks, and Celts. By the 6th century BC the Carthaginians had colonised much of southern Spain and were the most powerful group until they were ousted by the Romans who invaded. In 206 BC (the Second Punic War), then building paved roads, water systems, theatres and temples; some of the *fuentes* and washing areas still in use in the Sierra de Aracena are Roman. The region around **Minas de Río Tinto** (believed to be the oldest mines in the world) was developed by the Romans but is thought to have been established long before, and is believed by some to be the site of the mysterious and (so far) undiscovered city of Atlantis. Spain became the jewel in Rome's crown, bringing wealth and valuable trading links. **Andalucía** in particular developed wine, wool, olive oil and mining industries. When the Roman Empire collapsed, **Andalucía** was unprotected and open to barbarian attacks from various tribes, including the Vandals (thought to be the origin of the region's name (V)Andalucía) and the Visigoths who predominated in 458 AD, hanging on to power until Moors from North Africa and Arabia swept into Spain in 711.

A long period of Islamic dominance followed. At first Spain was governed from Baghdad, but later power was granted to the Moors running the country, until in the 10th century Abd ar-Rahamn 111 became Caliph of the Western Islamic Empire with **Córdoba** as its capital. Elegant mosques, palaces and buildings were erected, and a university system was established. Much of Spain's most beautiful architecture is Moorish. However, those following the Christian faith were repressed, resulting in uprisings. In the 13th century an organised Christian effort began, with some important successes such as the seizing of **Córdoba** and **Sevilla**. Even so, it wasn't until 1492 that the last Muslim stronghold fell in **Granada** and the Christian re-conquest was complete, headed by Isabel of Castille and Ferdinand of Aragon. But intolerance and repression were not the sole preserve of the Moors; the Christians began their own Inquisition, outlawing non-Christian religions and practices, destroying holy books and banning the speaking of Arabic; Jews and Muslims who wished to remain had to become Christians.

1492 was an eventful year, as Columbus made his famous journey from the port of **Huelva** to the Americas, bringing back riches of gold and silver. A period of wealth followed, but by the 17th century the Hapsburg kings of

Spain had spent huge amounts on waging European wars, coinciding with a spate of epidemics and failed harvests which hit **Andalucía** particularly hard, seriously reducing the population.

Things gradually improved until the end of the 18th century under the Bourbon dynasty (Spain's current royals can be traced back to them), when a programme of new town and road building was completed, and the ports of **Cádiz** and **Málaga** flourished. But then Louis XVI of France, (King Carlos 1V of Spain's cousin) was guillotined in 1793, so Spain attacked France. It was a disastrous campaign, resulting in French occupation of Spain under Napoleon. A further five year conflict began, successful this time for the Spanish, who asserted sovereignty, and drew up a new constitution.

One hundred years of struggle between Spain's liberals and conservatives began; while King Fernando V11 reigned (1814-1834) liberals were persecuted and the constitution torn up. The nation fell into a deep economic recession, then lost their American colonies to independence. Poverty amongst the lower classes was severe, particularly in **Andalucía**. Although the First Republic was announced by an incoming liberal government in 1873, it had lasted less than a year when the army reinstated the monarchy by force. A mass migration of poor Spanish desperate for a better life to South America followed, while groups of anarchists grew in strength and determination for radical change.

In 1931 elections brought in the Second Republic, and the King of the day, Alfonso X111 fled to Italy. The Second Republic lasted until 1936, when the frustration of groups of anarchists and fascists who were excluded from both the left and then the right wing governments of this period, exploded into the violence of the Spanish Civil War. The Nationalists (supported by Germany and Italy) took the cities and towns of **Andalucía**, leaving tens of thousands dead, and after a bitter and violent conflict which devastated the country, General Franco as leader of the Nationalists finally subdued the key cities of **Valencia**, **Madrid** and **Barcelona** at which time he declared himself leader of Spain on April 1 1939. Thirty-six years of repression followed, Franco's dictatorship filling jails with political prisoners, and allowing no political parties but his own *Movimento Nacional*. A trade boycott in 1940 further devastated Spain's already shaky economy, seriously affecting **Andalucía**. Another wave of some 1.5 million left the region, many heading for South America.

After Franco's death King Juan Carlos 11 became monarch but was determined to restore democracy, giving Spain back to its people and decentralising the government. He set up Autonomous Regions (**Andalucía** became autonomous in 1982) with their own regional administrations. Many laws have been relaxed in the decades since the dark days of Franco, and a robust multi-party system thrives; a tolerant, democratic society is now well established. **Andalucía** remains one of the poorer regions of Spain, suffering high levels of unemployment and in need of investment in its infrastructure. Improved roads and railways, and a welcome re-population are now under way, and tourism promises to bring an important boost to the economy of such regions as the **Sierra de Aracena**.

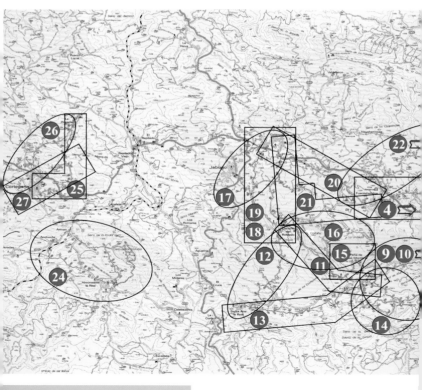

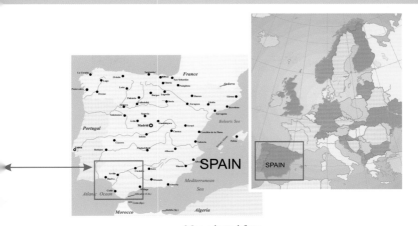

Map adapted from

Sierra de Aracena "Tour & Trail" Map

Published September 2004 by Discovery Walking Guides Ltd. Northampton NN5 7HJ England.
ISBN 1-899554-97-1 Copyright David & Ros Brawn September 2004

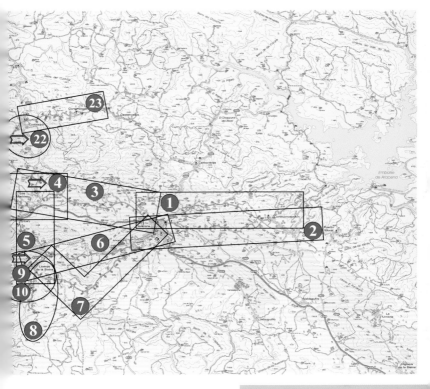

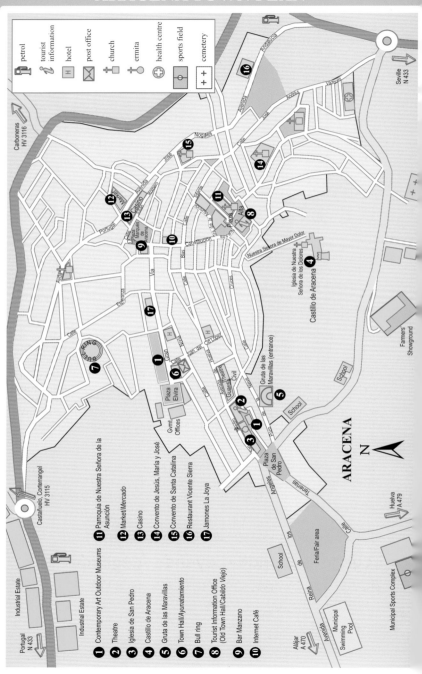

1. Contemporary Art Outdoor Museums
2. Theatre
3. Iglesia de San Pedro
4. Castillo de Aracena
5. Gruta de las Maravillas
6. Town Hall/Ayuntamiento
7. Bull ring
8. Tourist Information Office (Old Town Hall/Cabildo Viejo)
9. Bar Manzano
10. Internet Café
11. Parroquia de Nuestra Señora de la Asunción
12. Market/Mercado
13. Casino
14. Convento de Jesús, María y José
15. Convento de Santa Catalina
16. Restaurant Vicente Sierra
17. Jamones La Joya

ARACENA

N

petrol
tourist information
H hotel
⊠ post office
✝ church
♁ ermita
⊕ health centre
⬚ sports field
+ cemetery

Sierra de Aracena contains a great number of potential walking trails for the adventurous walker. In selecting our routes for this book we have given priority to the accessibility of routes, their attractiveness from a walking perspective, and the possibility of combining routes to make a circular days walking excursion. Even twenty seven walking routes is only scratching the surface of a region that is host to four *Gran Recorrido* (*GR*) long distance walking routes and some fifteen *Pequeño Recorrido* (*PR*) shorter walking routes. *GR* and *PR* routes are waymarked, some being recently 'repainted' while others seem to have been overlooked in the refurbishment. During our research we found two *PR* routes closed to navigation and suspect that only the recently painted waymarks indicate an open route.

The *GR* and *PR* routes are detailed in a general sketch map 'Walking Routes in the Sierra de Aracena and Pícos de Aroche' published by the **Huelva** tourist office and available from the tourist offices (free). 'Mapa Guía Sierra de Aracena y Pícos de Aroche' published by the **Aracena** local government and on sale at €4.50 provides more detail of *GR* and *PR* routes and includes 11 walking routes (in Spanish). 'Cuaderno de Senderos' is a walking booklet with very brief descriptions of 24 walking routes (in Spanish) on sale at the **Visitors' Centre**. 'Sierra de Aracena y Pícos de Aroche' is a 1:75,000 scale topographical map of the region on sale at the **Visitors' Centre**, though unfortunately the huge size of the single sided map makes it impractical for outdoor use.

Conventional topographic maps are available from Cartografía Militar de España; sheet 10-37 Aracena at 1:50,000 scale but it is seriously out of date (1994) in not showing the new N435 road. Servicio Geográfico del Ejército (CNIG) produce 1:50,000 scale and 1:25,000 scale topografical maps of the region which are more up to date than the military but few walking trails are shown on these maps. This could be because the maps are based upon aerial photography and many of the region's trails are hidden beneath tree cover. We did not find any shop stocking either the Militar or CNIG maps in the Sierra de Aracena region.

The map sections used in this book are taken from our Sierra de Aracena Tour & Trail Map at 1:40,000 scale (ISBN 1-899554-97-1 £2.99), which is based upon our GPS ground surveys carried out while researching the region during 2003 and 2004.

(For more details also see Appendices P.136, Maps & Books)

Legend-Legende-Leyenda-Légende
ROADS, STRAßE, CARRETERA, ROUTE

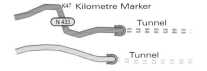

K47 Kilometre Marker

N 433

Tunnel

Main road, Hauptstraße, Carretera principal, Route à grande circulation

Tunnel

Secondary road, Regionalstraße, Carretera, Route

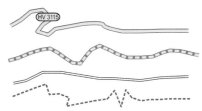

Minor road, Lokalstraße,
Carretera, Route secondaire

Narrow road, Fahrweg,
Camino Rural, Chemin carrosable

Dirt road, Fahrweg,
Camino, Chemin carrosable

Path, Fußweg, Sendero, Sentier

Walking Routes, Wanderweg, Sendero, Chemin.

Walking Route (Red) & Number

GPS Waypoint
see Sierra de Aracena guide book

17

Alternative Route (Green)

ALTITUDE, HÖHE, ALTITUD, ALTITUDE

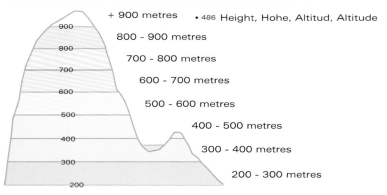

+ 900 metres   • 486 Height, Hohe, Altitud, Altitude

800 - 900 metres

700 - 800 metres

600 - 700 metres

500 - 600 metres

400 - 500 metres

300 - 400 metres

200 - 300 metres

SYMBOLS

Tower, Turm, Torre, Tour   ♦ Spring, Fuente   Hotel   Petrol

Church, Kirche, Iglesia, Église   Chapel, Kapelle, Ermita, Chapelle

Picnic area, Rastplatz, Zona Recreativa, Pique-nique

Cemetery, Friedhof, Cementario, Cimetière   Bar/Rest

Sports Ground, Sportplatz, Campo deportivo, Terrain de sport

Camping, Campingplatz, Camping, Camping   Bull Ring

Mirador   P Parking, Parkplatz   ⊤⊤ Seat by trail   Urban Area

Commercial Building   House

Important House   Ruin/Barn/Corral

3

our rating for effort/exertion:-
1 very easy   **2** easy   **3** average
4 energetic   **5** strenuous

approximate **time** to complete a walk (compare your times against ours early in a walk) - does not include stopping time

approximate walking **distance** in kilometres

 20m / 850m

approximate **ascents/descents** in metres (N = negligible)

circular route

linear route

risk of **vertigo**

refreshments (may be at start or end of a route only)

Walk descriptions include:

- timing in minutes, shown as (40M)
- compass directions, shown as (NW)
- heights in metres, shown as (1355m)
- GPS waypoints, shown as (Wp.3)

Notes on the text

Place names are shown in **bold text**, except where we refer to a written sign, when any place names are enclosed in single quotation marks.

Spanish words are shown in *italics*, and if also in *purple*, will be included in either the general glossary (P.127) or the food and drink glossary (P.23).

Waypost with plaque

In the spring of 2004 the Consejería de Medio Ambiente (the Regional Government's environment agency) completed the first phase of improvements in walking route sign boards and wayposts. Slim wooden waymarking posts sometimes carry a small plaque naming the route's start and finish points, while others confirm the route with an arrow. Although this is an excellent idea, we found that a number of posts were already damaged within weeks of their implantation, the plaques sometimes snapped off.

This confirms the need for accurate mapping, walk descriptions and GPS information if walkers are not to get lost.

Many of the routes criss-crossing the region are either *GR* or *PR* routes, part of a network linking across Europe. *Sendero de Gran Recorrido* routes are long distance trails (a minimum of 50 km in length) marked with red and white horizontal paint stripes, or sometimes with red and white incident tape. There are more than fifty such routes in Spain.

PR paint marks and direction waypost

Sendero de Pequeño Recorrido routes are shorter, indicated by yellow and white paint or tape. If you see a red and white or yellow and white diagonal cross, this means that you <u>don't</u> take this path. On some routes, both *GR* and *PR*, and on those that fit into neither category, you'll find old blobs of paint in 'discontinued' colours which can confuse, left over from old systems of waymarking. Waymarking is not an exact science.

Notice boards at the start of some routes, or at crossroads of trails, may give information about wildlife or plants in the area, or route details such as length and difficulty, though we've found these to vary in accuracy.

Information board on Walk 16

The GPS Waypoint lists provided in this **Sierra de Aracena - a Walk! Guidebook** by David & Ros Brawn, are as recorded by ourselves during our research of the 27 main walk descriptions contained in the book. In the interests of clarity, not all waypoints included in these lists are shown on the maps which accompany each detailed walk description.

 Waypoint Symbols

Where a Waypoint symbol is shown on a map, it has been placed alongside the position it refers to so as to not obscure the map detail, and is numbered so that it can be directly identified against the walk description and waypoint list. All of our GPS records were recorded using a Garmin 12XL which was clipped to David's backpack shoulder strap when it was not being carried in the hand.

All The GPS Waypoints quoted are subject to the general considerations as to the accuracy of GPS units in the location concerned. Sierra de Aracena has good GPS reception with little, if any, 'mountain shadowing' causing reception problems. We had anticipated reception problems in the narrow **Ribeira de Jabugo** valley (Walks 17 & 18) but our track records show a 3D level of accuracy. Even when we have been walking through woodland we did not suffer from 'trunk blocking', or 'leaf cover', reducing our satellite reception below the 3D level required for an accurate track record. Even on Walk 13, **Santa Ana la Real - Alájar** we recorded a good track record even though much of the route is through mature woodland beneath leaf cover.

In the narrow marble-cobbled streets of the Sierra de Aracena's towns, satellite reception is poor. We could get good signal strength in **Plaza del Marqués de Aracena** in the town of **Aracena**, but as soon as we move off through the narrow streets reception drops below the 3D level; sometimes dropping to nothing at all with the poor 12XL beeping away at us. **Linares de la Sierra**, **Alájar**, **Cortegana**, **Castaño del Robledo** and **Fuenteheridos** present similar reception problems depending upon the configuration of the satellites at the time that you are walking. The answer to this 'urban' problem is to use the walk description for navigation until you leave the narrow streets behind and acquire full satellite reception.

It is virtually impossible to reproduce the exact GPS Waypoint co-ordinates in practice when walking a route; unless you want to spend several minutes shuffling around until you reproduce the exact co-ordinates. While GPS Waypoints are quoted to 00.0001 minutes of arc, in practice you should expect 10 metres as an acceptable standard of accuracy when you have '3D navigation'(four or more satellites in view); though reception outside of the towns is good enough for your accuracy to be closer to 5 metres.

Signal Strength
Signal strength from sufficient satellites is crucial to obtaining an accurate location fix with your GPS unit. In open sky, ridge top, conditions you may

have up to 11 satellites in view to give you a GPS location accuracy of 5 metres. Providing you have good batteries, and wait until your GPS has full 'satellite acquisition' before starting out, your GPS will perform wonderfully in the Sierra de Aracena for all our country routes.

To Input the Waypoints
GPS Waypoint co-ordinates are quoted for the WGS84 datum, in degrees and minutes of Latitude and Longitude. To input the Waypoints into your GPS we suggest that you:

● Switch on your GPS and select 'simulator' mode.

● Check that your GPS is set to the WGS84 datum (its default datum) and the 'location format' 'hddd° .mm.mmm'.

● Input the GPS Waypoints into a 'route' file with the same number as the walking route number; then when you call up the 'route' in the Sierra de Aracena there will be no confusion as to which walking route it refers.

● Repeat the inputting of routes until you have covered all the routes you plan to walk, or until you have used up the memory capacity of your GPS; even the most basic of GPS units will store up to 20 routes of up to 50 Waypoints for each route, and you can always re-programme your GPS while in the Sierra de Aracena.

● Turn off your GPS. When you turn the GPS back on it should return to its normal navigation mode.

GPS Waypoints are provided as an additional navigation aid to complement the detailed walk descriptions in **Sierra de Aracena - a Walk! Guidebook.** Knowing exactly where you are in relation to our detailed walk description is a great confidence booster when exploring these new and exciting landscapes. GPS Waypoints are provided for all key navigational points on all walking routes; never again should you find yourself wondering whether you are on the right path or not.

Note that GPS Waypoints complement the detailed walking route descriptions, and are not intended as an alternative to those detailed descriptions.

Personal Navigator Files (PNFs) for the Sierra de Aracena

Full GPS track and waypoint records for the walking routes contained in **Sierra de Aracena - a Walk! Guidebook** are available from Discovery Walking Guides Ltd. They are included in our **Personal Navigator Files CD** which also includes GPS track and waypoint files for our walking routes in the **Alpujarras**, **Tenerife**, **Lanzarote**, **La Gomera**, **La Palma**, **Mallorca**, **Madeira**, **Menorca** and even a few UK walking routes from our UK research programme. Each annual PNF CD is available for £7.99 post paid. Files are supplied in Oziexplorer format, and you will need software compatible with this file format, such as GPSU and Gartrip, to be able to directly load the walking routes into your GPS. See our websites for latest PNF information.

Confused by GPS?

If you are confused by talk of GPS, but are interested in how this modern navigational aid could enhance your walking enjoyment then simply seek out a copy of **GPS The Easy Way**, the UK's best selling GPS manual. Written in an easy to read, lively, style and lavishly illustrated, **GPS The Easy Way** takes you through all aspects of GPS usage from absolute basics up to GPS Expert and debunking the myths about GPS along the way - an essential purchase for anyone thinking of buying a GPS.

"A compass points north"
but
"A GPS tells you where you are, where you have been, and can show you where you want to go."

"Ask not 'What is GPS?' - ask 'What can GPS do for me?' "

GPS The Easy Way is available from bookshops, outdoor shops, over the Internet, and post free from:

Discovery Walking Guides Ltd.
10 Tennyson Close
Northampton NN5 7HJ
www.walking.demon.co.uk & www.dwgwalking.co.uk

From reading the postings on uk.rec.walking internet news group, it's obvious that walkers are very interested in the clothing and equipment used by other walkers. For some, this interest borders on obsession, with heated debates over walking poles, boots versus sandals, GPS versus 'map and compass' navigation etc. etc. Walking magazines are packed with clothing and equipment reviews, opinions and adverts, but few walking guide books give more than a cursory mention to recommended clothing and equipment.

Sierra de Aracena is a pastoral landscape of valleys, folded ridges and some plains; similar in nature to some popular UK walking regions and your UK equipment should be sufficient for all of our walking routes subject to a few useful additions.

At the risk of upsetting some walking fundamentalists, here is a brief rundown on what we've used on our adventures around the Sierra de Aracena.

BACKPACK

A 25-30 litre day pack should easily cope with all the equipment you think you will need for a day's walking. A design with plenty of outside pockets to give easy access to frequently used items, such as ½litre water bottles, is a good starting point. Well padded straps will spread the load and a waist strap will stop the pack moving about on the more adventurous routes. A ventilated back panel will help clear sweat on hot days and tough routes; a design with a stand-off frame is best for ventilation and worth the small increase in weight. Do spend time adjusting the straps so that you get the most comfortable fit.

As an alternative to traditional backpack designs, you might find the cyclists' packs produced by **Nikko** (which we use), and similar companies, a good compromise of stand-off frame, capacity, pockets and weight.

FOOTWEAR

Our Sierra de Aracena underfoot conditions range from a little stretch on pavements and tarmac roads, moving off onto comfortable dirt tracks and walking trails. The trails range from well-cobbled donkey trails, some dating back to Roman times, which can be slippery when wet, to sections which have suffered from water erosion. On some ford crossings you might be happier wading across rather than risking the 'stepping stones'.

Whether you choose boots, shoes or sandals they must be up to the task. You will need a good sole with plenty of grip and a well padded foot-bed. After wearing my **Bestard Race K** shoes on the first day David 'down graded' to softer **Berghaus** mesh walking shoes for most routes. Ros completed all the routes in sandals, alternating between her **Merrell**, good wet grip, and **Cats**, good on hard rock, designs.

On some routes brambles are rather intrusive and you might feel better protected with long socks, and even gaiters might make sense in some circumstances.

Whichever footwear you choose, do make sure that you have covered plenty of kilometres in them before coming to Sierra de Aracena.

SUN PROTECTION

Sierra de Aracena does not have the sunshine reputation of many of our walking destinations but you should not ignore protection from the sun; particularly in the summer months. Wear comfortable loose clothing and always carry a comfortable sun hat. Choose a design that gives you plenty of shade, is comfortable to wear, and stays on your head in windy conditions; our choice is the **Rohan** 'Legionnaire' style which protects neck and ears. You will be spending several hours a day outdoors and sunburnt ears (and neck) are both painful and embarrassing. Use a high-factor sun cream on all exposed skin.

We favour wrap-round sunglasses for eye protection.

Much of our walking is through mature woodland providing welcoming shade on hot days and cooler places to take a break; though most of the wooden 'log' seats we refer to in the descriptions are in the open.

WATER & FOOD

Dehydration is always a danger for energetic walkers even in these comparatively benign landscapes.

Always carry as much water as you think you might drink. A couple of ½ litre bottles, a few pence each from local shops, is the minimum, and add extra in hot weather.

While we tend to walk from village to village, aiming to finish in a *tipico* bar/cafe we would advise that you carry some survival rations. Rural *tipico* bar/restaurants are mostly friendly establishments, so please use them as refreshment stops and not just for the toilets.

WET WEATHER

There is a reason why the Sierra de Aracena has lush vegetation and many watercourses - rain. As we always walk in shorts when the weather is warm enough, our rain protection consists of lightweight waterproof jackets carried in our backpacks. Whenever we've been caught by the rain in the Sierra de Aracena, it has happened in calm conditions, the dark sky simply emptying straight down on our heads. In these comparatively windless conditions an umbrella becomes a viable and comfortable alternative to traditional walking wet weather gear.

MEDICAL KIT

Antiseptic wipes, antiseptic cream, plasters and bandage are supplemented by lip salve and tweezers. If you are walking with bare arms and legs then some scratches are likely. When you notice these use antiseptic wipes to clean and then antiseptic cream. Do not wash these scratches in local water courses; some are almost potable but others are certainly not. A whistle and a mobile phone just in case you have a once in a lifetime emergency; we've never had to use ours yet.

NAVIGATION

Do not compromise - buy the best guide book and the best map, and carry them with you. A compass is useful to orientate yourself at the start of a route and for general directions, but a GPS unit is far more useful; particularly if you are inputting our waypoints or downloading our PNF files, after which navigation is a doddle.

CLOTHING

Choose loose comfortable clothing and add a lightweight waterproof jacket to your back pack. Our 'research work'wear is very simple; cap sleeve and polo shirts, standard walking shorts which David 'cuts off' so the legs end above the knee, standard underwear etc. Only when it comes to footwear and headgear do we insist on something special.

OTHER EQUIPMENT

One piece of equipment that should be ready for use while walking in the Sierra de Aracena is a pair of secateurs. How much easier to snip off intrusive twigs and brambles to leave the route in better condition than you found it. Lightweight binoculars can be useful, or a monocular which is neater and lighter. Similarly digital cameras usually weigh far less than their film equivalents, and you are not committed to processing costs unless you want to run off prints. Some Euro notes in a secure pocket, and that's us off into adventuring around the Sierra de Aracena.

This was our first ever walk in the Sierra de Aracena, when we combined it with Walk 2 for a pleasant day's exploring, complete with two welcoming bars in **Corteconcepción** for refreshments. It's still one of our favourite walks as it combines many of the region's virtues without excessive exertion, making it a good introduction to the pleasures of the Sierra de Aracena.

Our starting point is in **Aracena**'s central square, **Plaza del Marqués de Aracena** (Wp.1 0M) from where we head up past the **Casino de Arias Montano** on **Calle Mesónes** to pass the old nunnery before swinging right past the **Centro Paroquial**, the **Ermita de la Señora Reina de Los Angeles** coming into view as we keep ascending the steep streets. Passing the *ermita* (Wp.2 5M), we go through the tunnel under the **Aracena** N433 bypass to emerge on a minor road which, after the steep climb so far, thankfully runs steadily downhill to a narrow tarmac lane off to the right (ENE Wp.3 12M) with a *PR* waymark and sign board 'Aracena - Corteconcepción arroyo 4.8 Kilometres 2 Hours med/low difficulty'.

As we head out on the narrow lane, the tarmac gives way to cobbles, then concrete and finally dirt as our track winds through a bucolic landscape, beautiful at any time of year but stunning in spring with its sparkling wild flowers. Our track gently descends between olives and rock banks to pass a track off to the right by a waypost and shrine, and come to **El Guindal** farm with its noisy dogs (Wp.4 18M). We stroll along, elevated above the valley floor, cork oaks overhanging the track as we pass a seat and come to a second signboard at a junction (Wp.5 22M).

Keeping to the main track, we climb up alongside a stone wall to go over a crest, and then drop down past a piggery/chicken farm and a *PR* waymark by a farm entrance, a track going right to the **Tierra Esperanza** *communidad* visible across the valley from us, its neat appearance a contrast to the farm buildings we've been passing. We come down past **Los García** farm (Wp.6) on our right, our track steepening into a near knee-jarring descent before passing **La Pastora** on our right (Wp.7) when the gradient eases to a gentle

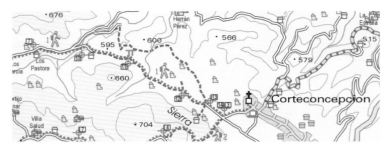

downhill. The sound of rushing water rises up to us as we pass a waterfall (Wp.8 40M) just before a fork in the track (Wp.9) where a waypost directs us down to the right to cross the stream of **Arroyo de la Fuente del Rey** assisted by stepping stones and wooden handrail (Wp.10 43M).

The stepped walking trail

Up from the stream we pass a house with noisy dogs, and continue up a broad trail which narrows to a stepped walking trail for us to steadily climb up over a crest, then resume our strolling between oak meadows and pollarded chestnuts to reach a seat by a gate entrance (Wp.11 54M).

At the seat our trail turns sharp right (SE) to push through foliage which threatens to overwhelm the path (secateurs useful) before we cross a water course, our trail widening to donkey trail width as it climbs past a waypost and *PR* waymark. Now our route levels out, and we are walking between groves of olives. We pass field entrances, our trail gradually widening (the trail is probably driveable by a small tractor from the seat we passed at 54 minutes, so technically this is a track) as we pass between low stone walls to a junction (Wp.12) where an overgrown path goes left; probably so overgrown as to be impassable.

Our track becomes rougher as we pass more field entrances in a gentle ascent, up to a 'tiled' sign at a three-way junction (Wp.13 67M); a track to the left (WNW), ahead is signed 'Corteconcepción', the route we've just come along is signed 'Fuente del Rei', while to the right is 'Carboneros, Los Molinos'. We continue ahead.

Corteconcepción comes into view ahead as we come down to another junction (Wp.14 72M); 'Corteconcepción' signed left, 'Carboneras' the way we have come, and 'Aracena, Rebollar' signed right, while an unmarked track straight ahead. Going left (NE), the walls become better built as we stroll past small holdings and olives while heading towards the church tower which dominates the skyline ahead. The track becomes cobbled and now turns into a 'traffic free' village street for us to stroll past terraced houses to come into the neat town square, complete with seating and bar. Going left, we walk up past **Hostal Casa del Cura** (closed whenever we've been passing), to the upper square in front of the church of **Corteconcepción**. (Wp.15 78M).

After admiring the old church, and much newer sundial, we seek out refreshment. On the corner of the lower square is a welcoming *tipico* with the large hearth typical of traditional bars in the region. Heading down the 'main' street, we come across a modern but no less welcoming bar, giving a choice of refreshments in this 'end of the road' town.

If you've arrived in **Corteconcepción** by following Walk 1, then this route is your logical return to **Aracena**. It's quite different in nature; a stiff climb just after the start is followed by a stroll through cattle country on a broad dirt track that runs along the high ground giving good views, before running down to the outskirts of **Aracena**.

Access by Car
Corteconcepción has comparatively wide concrete streets which usually have plenty of on-street parking available. Should everybody be at home, then either park towards the lower end of the village, or outside and walk in/up to our start point outside the church.

Starting from **Corteconcepción**'s impressive church (Wp.1 0M) and sundial (installed 1988), we walk down past **Hostal del Cura** to turn right into the pretty square where we take the concrete street from its north-east corner (Walk 1 in reverse). We follow the street to the end of the houses (Wp.2), where our route continues ahead as an easy-strolling track to bring us to a crossroads of the ways (Wp.3 5M); Walk 1 comes in from the right, while we go straight ahead on the 'Aracena, Rebollar' signed trail.

We are on an old stone-laid donkey trail which climbs between stone walls towards the ridge ahead; yes, there is 'some' climbing to come.

... below a fence-topped stone wall, ...

It's a steady grinding ascent, coming under cork oaks as we ascend and taking breaks whenever needed. Once a 'main' commuting route to and from the regional capital, since the arrival of tarmac roads this trail is little used except by leisure walkers like us, though most of it stays in good condition thanks to the stone steps which protect the cobbling from water erosion. We come up to walk below a fence-topped stone wall, the trail now rather eroded as we continue ascending, the excellent views behind us justifying our rest breaks in the climb. Eventually we come up to the grand entrance to the fenced property (Wp.4 20M) and step onto a dirt track.

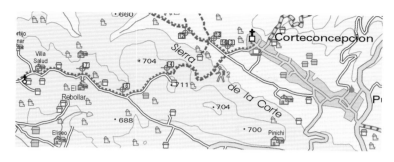

After that almost relentless ascent, we deserve something easy as we now stroll along the track between cork oaks and olive groves to run gently downhill to a smelly chicken farm (Wp.5), which we pass quickly to come through the trees to the unusual sight of a '40 km' speed limit sign beside a dirt road (Wp.6 28M) - perhaps not so unusual when some official maps show this as a tarmacked minor road. Minor road it certainly is, but they've forgotten to tarmac it. Turning right, we stroll along the road (ENE), route confirmed by *PR* waymarking, passing a pond with pigs, geese and ducks in residence which sets the tone for our idyllic rural route.

We stay on the broad dirt road for two kilometres of comfortable, easy walking along a broad spine allowing extensive views to both south and north. Rather than bore you with directions, simply look out for the entrance to **El Rebollar** (Wp.7 35M), its massive bulls resting on their assets, 'Joseph Thomson at home' (Wp.8), a dirt road (N) to **Cortijo Pinar** (Wp.9), another entrance to **El Rebollar** (Wp.10, and obviously a big property), until we come to a junction by a large chicken farm on the right (Wp.11 63M); here a dirt road goes left (S) and a donkey trail front left (ESE), while the main dirt road continues ahead (E). Now we have a choice of two finishes.

The easier finish
Our 'official' *PR* route leaves the main dirt road at this point on the donkey trail, but you have an alternative. If you stay on the main dirt road for another kilometre it will take you along past the **Ermita de San Roque** to the N433 **Aracena** bypass. Carefully crossing the bypass you come down into the edge of **Aracena** by the **Ermita de Nuestra Señora Reina de Los Angeles**, from where it's an easy downhill stroll to the town's central plaza, an easy and comfortable finish.

The more challenging finish
By comparison our 'official' *PR* route is a little more challenging. From the junction (Wp.11) we go left onto the dirt track, and then right to take a smaller track which starts climbing up past a house entrance (Wp.12). Our track becomes rougher and less used as we climb steadily, 'relentless' might be on the tip of your tongue, but after passing a track off to our left and a final steep section, we do reach the crest by a three-way field entrance.

Aracena comes into view as our track dwindles to a trail, badly eroded so making for a picky descent until we come to the gates of **La Era 2001** (Wp.13 72M) where we return to a narrow track which descends towards the town. An easy stroll along the elevated track brings us onto a steep descent to join the concrete lane which serves the transmitter towers on top of the ridge, from where we meet and carefully cross over the N433.

To access the town's streets, we need to walk back to the first street (Wp.14), opposite our track, and joined to it in pre-bypass days, to head down into the town. We descend towards the unfinished **Iglesia de la Asunción**, crossing a tarmac road and then turning right to pass another church, following a narrow cobbled street downhill. At the end of the narrow street we turn right to come onto the central square of **Plaza del Marqués de Aracena** (Wp.15 Note that there is usually poor GPS reception in the narrow streets, and this waypoint is only to make sure you find **Bar Manzano** (87M).

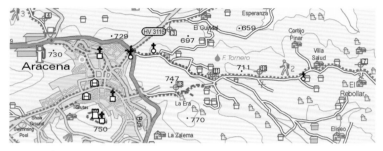

3 ARACENA - LOS MARINES

A classic route through beautiful countryside linking the regional capital with the pretty village of **Los Marines**. Once we've climbed out of the town, it is all easy strolling through chestnut groves, farms and small holdings on well made tracks and trails, before a short stretch of tarmac road takes us into the village. If you park at the small industrial estate by the roundabout north of **Aracena** you can enjoy easy strolling, and reduce the walk rating to 2 Walkers.

Although this route is one of the easiest physically, we do negotiate quite a maze of tracks and trails, not helped by old waymarking which can tempt you onto old routes that have now disappeared. Keep to our description if you want to arrive at **Los Marines** in two hours. A compass is useful to keep you on the correct general heading; GPS users will find the waypoints a boon, and should you be using our PNF file on your GPS, then navigation is a doddle!

Access by Bus
Make your way north-west from **Aracena** bus station to the central square of **Plaza del Marqués de Aracena**, or to the **Hotel Sierra de Aracena** for an alternative start.

Access by Car
If you park on the industrial estate near Wp.3 you'll avoid the slogging climb out of **Aracena**.

We start out from the north-west corner of the central **Plaza del Marqués de Aracena** (Wp.1 0M) to take the side street up past the Tabac shop. At the top of the street we join the tarmacked old main road to go left, following the 'Portugal' sign, and climb up past the **Iglesia de Santa Lucía** (Wp.2) and keep slogging up the pavements until they run out at scruffy workshops, where we walk up the side of the road to carefully cross the N433 at the roundabout. After that energetic ascent you might feel that you have earned at least a coffee in **Mesón la Reja** (Wp.3 14M).

Alternative start
If you are staying in **Aracena**, then you might like a cobbled alternative to the old main road ascent. From outside **Hotel Sierra de Aracena**, take the side street heading north and keep heading roughly north to the **Plaza de Toros** (bull ring), then it is north-west up the narrow streets to join the 'main road' before the workshops. More artesanial but no less of a climb.

The industrial estate seems an unlikely setting for a beautiful walk as we set off up the track (N) at the side of **Mesón La Reja**, but over a crest we come down to a signboard (Wp.4) 'Aracena - Fuenteheridos 10.5 kilometres 3.5 hours medium difficulty'. For the first stage of our route we simply stay on the main track and avoid the temptation of side tracks, not as easy as it sounds with the confusing waymarking in this region. Our track runs downhill

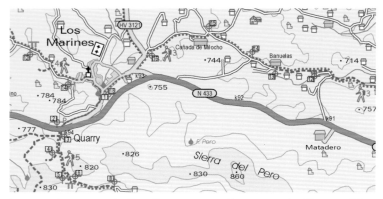

between chestnuts and olives for an easy stroll, past a track off to our right. Chestnut groves take over both sides of our route as we come past a house set amongst the trees, and then the track swings right in front of a farmstead, the track levelling out to bring us to a junction (Wp.5 26M) and our first temptation.

A track, equally significant as the one we're on, goes right (N) and it has *PR* and *GR* waymarks, and there's a waymarking post. One of the routes to which the waymarks refer disappeared some time ago when a river bridge was swept away, but nobody has removed the old marks. Keeping straight on (NE), we stroll along in the dappled shade from the old trees lining the track, swinging west as we pass a farmstead set off amongst the trees on the right. Next is a track off to our right (Wp.6 31M), while our track has *GR* marking both sides of the junction as we continue west (W), going gently uphill between stone walls to pass a farmstead and a 'Carril Cortado' (lane closed) track on our right. Our route has been gradually swinging south-west to bring us to a track (Wp.7 37M) off to our left (S); again, there's a waypost and the track has *PR* and *GR* markings. Do not be tempted, as the track now leads to a private house and the old *sendero* walking trail (PRA47) has become overgrown.

Keeping on the main track (W) we are soon at the next junction (Wp.8 41M) where the track to the right has a *PR* mark; originally this linked to Wp.5 in a loop taking in the **Caños** but now cut since the bridge washed away. Continuing uphill (W) we pass a waypost and a minor track off to our left and then an overgrown donkey trail, as we start an ascent to pass between a pink farmstead and a ruin (Wp.9). There are two more farmsteads away on our right before we come up to a crest, our track narrowing and becoming rougher as it brings us down to an old barn (Wp.10 51M). Our track/trail skitters down to a gurgling stream creating a wet area, almost a marsh, which we negotiate to reach a track junction (Wp.11) where a red arrow directs us west while another track climbs to the south.

We come up to a waypost and *GR* mark by a 'Sin Salida' (no exit) track off to our right and continue on (W) to a split in the track where we keep to the trail/track on the right of the main track which runs up to a house (Wp.12). Unfortunately, the trail/track also acts as a water runoff making for rough going to pass a second house on our left, the countryside noticeably changing from chestnuts to cork oaks and olives as we come towards industrial style

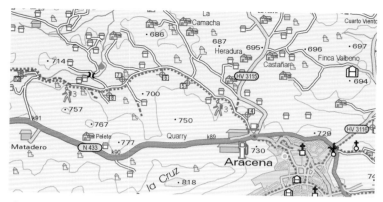

farm buildings. At the buildings, we come onto a better track that serves the farm and has a *GR* mark (Wp.13 72M). We are back to comfortable walking, passing a minor track off to our left as we head into this pastoral landscape.

We stay on the main track only until we come to a farmhouse (Wp.14 76M) where the track goes left up to the N433, while we go straight ahead on a little-used track marked with a waypost and a faint arrow on an oak tree. Our much-eroded track climbs up through oaks and chestnuts to a crest, before running down to pass a white house, bringing us onto a better stabilised track at a crossroads (Wp.15 85M); the new track is so well stabilised that it's actually tarmacked at this point. Although the *GR* marking appears to indicate the road ahead, this is actually a longer alternative route, while we go left on the main track to swing west and stroll past another industrial farm, **Cañada del Milocho**.

Again, the rule is to stay on the main track and not to be tempted either by the farm's access roads, or by the dirt track which goes right to link to Wp.15, or by another track right - but keep straight on to come out of the trees to meet the **Cortelazor** road (Wp.16 96M). Now the wayfinding problems are behind us as we walk up the tarmac (SW) to pass noisy dogs guarding a building on the right before coming to a junction (Wp.17) just east of **Los Marines**.

Going right, we stroll down what was the old main road, now bypassed by the N433, with its mix of new and traditional houses (but no bar!) to the public washing area (Wp.18 105M). Here we take the cobbled street into the little town heading for the church tower, passing (!) **Bar Marsalino** as we head up to take a steeper street to our left, and a final climb brings us onto the pretty square below the church and another bar. If you are continuing on to **Fuenteheridos** (Walk 4 in reverse), then continue up the street past the church; but we will divert right into the bar's cool interior to partake of refreshment.

Los Marines church square

This pleasant country walk also links to the walks out of both these small towns, giving lots of alternative route combinations. Considering that both towns are at similar altitude. this route is rather energetic as we toil up a long ridge climb to a well-sited log seat, before continuing to **Los Marines**. Fans of waymarking should be well satisfied, as this is one of the most marked routes in the region with its carved wood *sendero* signs complementing the frequent *GR* posts and route signboards.

Access by Car

Turn off the N433 at the over-complicated **Fuenteheridos** junction and head up to the town to see if it is possible to park either around the square (unlikely) or on the road onto the square; possibly. Alternatively, park at the large car park of **Hotel Villa Turistica Fuenteheridos** or (most imaginatively) drive the narrow cobbled street at the start of the walking route and park opposite the football ground at Wp.2.

> **Short Walk Option**
> Stay on the track at Wp.5 by **Finca la Deseada** to wind along the northern side of the valley, joining our Fuenteheridos-Cortelazor route at its Wp.8, then follow that route in reverse back to the N433.

If starting from the **Villa Turistica** you'll find it easiest to walk along the N433 main road to join the route at Wp.3.

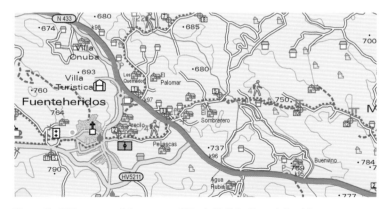

From the NE corner of the square (Wp.1 0M) in **Fuenteheridos** we put our back to the famous **12 Pipes** *fuente* and walk up a steep cobbled street. Slogging up past the last of the houses, the street passes through green gates, apparently always open, and levels out to pass in front of the football pitch (Wp.2) and a walled modern bungalow (?) to continue as a dirt track.

Before heading down the track, take a minute while at this elevated position, to look over the landscape that we'll be walking through; wooded valleys and ridges, with just the occasional house visible. The dirt track runs down from the plateau to cross a stream before contouring above a valley, passing the entrance of **Las Peûascas**, then dropping steeply down for us to meet the N433 by a *GR* post (Wp.3 13M).

Across the main road, we walk down the track's continuation past the 'Fuenteheridos - Aracena 10.5 km 3.5 hrs' signboard and a *GR* waymark. Keeping to the main track, we pass a number of entrances as we stroll gently downhill through the pleasant countryside before passing **Hacienda el Sombrerero**, an unusual house with a raised roof creating a concert hall effect.

A track goes left at a junction (Wp.4 20M) while we keep right, sauntering along between chestnuts, cork oaks and fruit trees to the entrance of **Finca la Deseada** (Wp.5 23M) where a narrow trail is signed and has *GR* waymarking; in this relaxed atmosphere walkers can easily come to grief by missing this junction and continuing on the easy track which meets with our **Cortelazor** route - if you get through the northern tangle of tracks!

Taking the narrow trail alongside **Finca La Deseada**, we meander beside fruit trees before dropping down to a stream crossing (Wp.6) in a green tunnel. From the stream, we start to climb past a new house and come to a *GR* post (Wp.7) where a dirt track crosses our route. Our narrow trail parallels the house's access track and crosses a private entrance before we come to a *casa rural* holiday house (Wp.8 35M).

Now we leave the houses behind as we start a steady ascent up from the **Buenvino** valley, passing a *GR* post, our trail becoming stonier as we climb higher amongst the cork oaks.

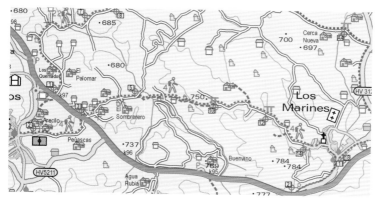

We come up to overlook a barn (Wp.9) which is home to two over-friendly large 'herd' dogs who are big enough to bar our path, not so friendly if you see them at work with their flock. After our canine interlude it is onwards and upwards in a relentless ascent through the trees, coming into the open for a final steep ascent up to a thoughtfully sited log seat (Wp.10 47M) set on the top of a cleared ridge beside a dirt track and wooden signboard.

After an almost compulsory break on the seat we set off down the track through an area partially cleared of trees. We pass four *GR* posts on this easy strolling section before coming down to a junction (Wp.11) with another carved wood *sendero* sign and post where a minor track drops down into the valley on our left; a *GR* waymark indicates a left turn for walkers arriving from **Los Marines**.

Keeping right on the main track, we have a steep climb up out of the valley, passing a track off to our right and an interesting rock formation, also on our right, before reaching the crest by a stone seat set below a cork oak (Wp.12); most thoughtful.

... an interesting rock formation ...

After the stone seat our track runs (thankfully) downhill to pass a modern house (Wp.13) as the houses of **Los Marines** come into view. We come down past olive groves and a *horno de calc* oven to a waymarking sign for **Aracena** (Wp.14 70M) just before the first house, Nº20A, where we come onto a cobbled street. Immediately we reach a junction where we head downhill to a *fuente* T-junction. Ahead is the church's brilliant blue and white tiled spire as we go right - left is a cul-de-sac - to come down to the Italianate **Iglesia de Santa María de Gracia** (Wp.15 75M). Behind the church is the town square with seating and the **Mesón Carlos** for refreshments.

5 LOS MARINES - LINARES DE LA SIERRA

When walking in the Sierra de Aracena, we often find ourselves amongst woodland or in valleys which restrict the views, but this route gives us views in abundance, as we cross the high pass between **Los Marines** and **Linares de la Sierra**. Even if you don't plan to do the full route, take our Short Walk option to see the spectacular views from the pass.

The first part of our route to the views from the pass on top of the *sierra* is a popular 'Sunday Stroll' for the locals, while the full route with its long descent into **Linares de la Sierra** is more the preserve of 'booted' visitors.

Access by Car
Turn off the N433 at the **Los Marines** junction (east or west) and park on the old main road near the public wash area, or west of **Los Marines** where a piece of the old main road makes a tarmacked parking area opposite the large quarry.

> **Short Walk**
> To the pass and return. 2 Walker. 45 minutes there and back.

Our start point is from the **Los Marines** *lavadero* and its statue (Wp.1 0M), to walk up the old main road (SW) past the 'El Castaña' signboard and the 'spouting pipes', the local equivalent of the **Fuente de los Doce Caños** of **Fuenteheridos** - perhaps not as impressive, but still interesting when they are 'spouting'. It is gently uphill between forested slopes to come to the N433 junction, where we continue on the old tarmac across the parking area. We cross the main road at the end of the massive quarry (Wp.2 8M) and come onto the trail and the 'Los Marines - Alto del Chorrito' sign board (3 Kilometres, 1 Hour, 110 metres of ascents), though by our calculation and timings it is only 60 metres of ascents and 45 minutes at our normal walking speed.

At first an old cobbled donkey trail leads us into the forested slopes, but where the donkey trail goes right (Wp.3), we continue straight ahead (S) on a walking trail marked by a waypost and *PR* mark. The massive quarry is only a stone's throw away, and the main road to Portugal is just behind us, but on this old trail amongst these green forested slopes, we could be an age away. We come up to a junction with a waypost (Wp.4), where we keep left to start climbing in earnest along the cobbled trail between oaks and chestnuts. Bracken lines our climb, and the cobbles are softened by a covering of chestnut husks as we ascend to a pylon and an 'Umbrias y Solanas' signboard (Wp.5 18M), explaining in Spanish the difference between the northern 'umbrias' and southern 'solanas'. The signboard and pylon mark the high point of our route, though if you are taking our Short Walk option, you should continue a little further to the log seat for better views.

From the pass, we emerge from the trees to look out over the southern *sierras*.

... wonderful views en route to Linares de la Sierra ...

Now it's all downhill, and what a downhill it is, as the *sierra* slopes steeply down to the river valleys. We set off down the trail as it starts a long traverse (ESE) across the steep slope, possibly tempted by a log seat (Wp.6 and end of Short Walk), our trail running alongside a low stone wall for us to pass the remains of a signboard (Wp.7 23M)

Unfortunately the cobbled base of the trail is now littered with loose stone carried onto the trail by storm waters; this, combined with pushing through the vegetation, makes for a rather picky descent before we emerge onto a turn in a dirt track (Wp.8 32M). A red cross waymark on the left shows that we should head downhill - as if we would think of anything else.

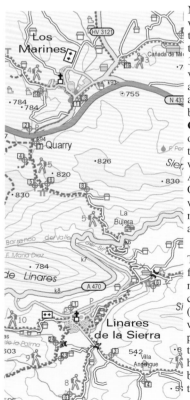

Now we have the luxury of the broad, well-stabilised track allowing us to take in the views as we head downhill to a *mirador* turn in the track (Wp.9 37M) deserving of a 'drink in the views' break. The track swings back and forth, always downhill, giving alternating views of the valleys and back towards the pylon at the **Alto del Chorrito** - this illustrates the scale of our descent so far. At a steeper section the track has been concreted, and widens out to almost road width as the A470 road comes into view below us. Our track reverts to dirt shortly before we curve down to the 'main' road, marked with a red arrow up the track and *PR* and *GR* marks.

Turning right, we cross the road to face any oncoming traffic and in fifty metres we come to the track's continuation marked with red arrows (Wp.10 45M) and a variety of waymarks. Down past a smelly pig pen and a *PR* waymark, we drop into the **Linares de la Sierra** valley, the hairpin bends protected by crash barriers showing that this was the town's access road until recently.

After zigzagging down through the

oaks, we come to a junction (Wp.11) where another track comes down from our left, and then it's back to zigzagging down towards a pair of houses. We pass the entrance to **Valle San Juan** alongside a track off to our left as we swing right to pass a small waterfall (Wp.12), our route crossing the stream and levelling out as we approach the houses seen earlier. After the first house of **S'João**, a little rise takes us past the second house to a T-junction below the entrance to **La Herreria** (Wp.13 62M), and a waypost has an arrow pointing downhill to our left plus *PR* waymark on a wall. (Note that down here in the lower valley amongst the trees, GPS reception is relatively poor, giving an approximate accuracy of 20 metres.)

At the T-junction we keep right for **Linares de la Sierra**, but if you are linking this route to Walk 6 for **Aracena**, then you can go left and forgo **Linares**, saving approximately 30 minutes from the combined times of the two routes.

Heading west along the track we come to a *fuente* and drinking troughs, just after which we leave the track on a trail (Wp.14) marked by a waypost and *PR* waymark. We come down an eroded cobbled trail between steep walls before curving above animal pens, our route confirmed by waypost and waymarks. Our trail clings to the valley wall as the valley gets steeper before we come to a waypost (Wp.15) marking a split in the trail. Taking the upper trail as it widens to a track brings us to the first of the houses of **Linares** houses, and we continue downhill to meet the first cobbled streets (Wp.16). Turning right, we ascend the steep cobbled street to meet the main street by the 'Linares - Aracena' sign. Turning left, we now have an easy stroll (W) along to the **Plaza de Toros** sited below the church (Wp.17 85M), where we can take refreshments at the unusual bar, seated outside in the bull ring, or inside behind the barred doors if a fight is in progress.

Linares de la Sierra sits deep in the valleys of the *sierras*, which means that if you want to take the shortest and most direct route to the next town, you have to cross one of the high ridges. This is the direct route to **Aracena** that was the 'donkey trail motorway' of the region until the A470 road was built. 'Direct' means that we have a relentless ascent of two hundred metres before crossing the pass, after which it is comparatively gentle strolling on the second half of our route to the outskirts of **Aracena**.

For a less physically challenging but longer route between the two towns, take Walk 7.

4   2 H   7½ km   190m / 40m   4*

* in **Aracena**

Access by Car
Park along the access road above the town and walk down to the bull ring below the church.

Short Walk Option
Follow our main route out to the seat at Wp.6, a rather pleasant spot for a picnic, and return along the track and tarmac of our Alternative Start. (30 minutes)

The steep cobbled street at Wp.2

As we leave the **Plaza de Toros** bullring bar in **Linares de la Sierra** (Wp.1 0M), it's almost impossible not to scuff our boots in the sand while adopting a matador's swagger before we stride out of the open gates and turn left. We follow the main street (E) along to the edge of town (Wp.2), where we turn down the cobbled street with the 'Linares - Aracena' signboard. A sinuous descent through the houses on the cobbles brings us to a junction (Wp.3) where we go left (NE) on a dirt track which narrows to a trail after the last house.

Our trail clings to the steep valley wall revealing picturesque vistas of this rural idyll as we steadily climb, a steeper climb up between walls bringing us onto a well-stabilised track by a *fuente* and drinking trough (Wp.4), from where we continue east to a T-junction (Wp.5 14M).

Alternative start
If you prefer tarmac and track to exciting trails, you could reach Wp.4 by simply continuing out of town on the tarmac access road, keeping east at the junction and then taking the first track on the right.

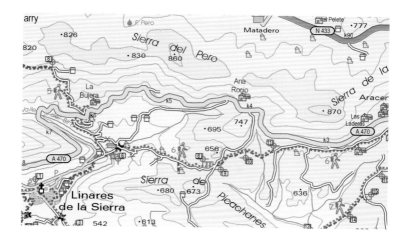

We go right at the T-junction for a skittery descent down to a log seat set beside a stream crossing beneath the trees (Wp.6). Across the stream, our track climbs up through the trees alongside a tumbling stream, reaching a waypost and a bridge over the stream at a junction (Wp.7). We cross the bridge to go uphill past a building and continue up alongside a stream in a 'puff and grunt' ascent. This is one long, almost relentless, ascent up to the pass, so take pleasure in the surroundings such as pools in the stream formed by layers of rock, the thoughtful concreting of the steeper sections, the bucolic woodland pastures; in short almost anything to stop thinking about the ascent.

Our track varies between steep, steeper, and not quite so steep, with good views back to the church in **Linares de la Sierra** when we take a break in the ascent. We climb up past field entrances, a distant *cortijo* across the valley, a path to a ruin, and some *PR* waymarks - and just as we are dreaming of a log seat to sit down on, one materialises ahead of us alongside the track (Wp.8 42M and 642 metres altitude). This is a beautiful wooded valley, if perhaps a trifle steep, which we have probably not seen in the best of lights while the sweat of the ascent was running into our eyes, so we recommend (!) a break on the seat to take in the beauty around us lest we leave this place with the wrong image in our mind.

From the seat it is still uphill to a T-junction (Wp.9) with a flat track that runs across to the A470 road. Across the track a waypost and waymarking indicate a walking trail running through the woods in a gentle climb, more PR waymarking confirming our route as we stroll through the trees and shrubs to a second waypost opposite a gate entrance (Wp.10). This also marks the high point of our trail, as we wind downhill on the eroded path to another waypost by a water runoff, and then it's uphill once again, the trail's original boulder-laid surface now all but eliminated by water erosion and lack of maintenance. We come onto a track marked by a waypost and signed back to 'Linares' the way we have come (Wp.11).

Turning left, we walk along the track with views out over the southern *sierras* while the steep slopes up to **San Ginés** dominate the northern aspect. We face

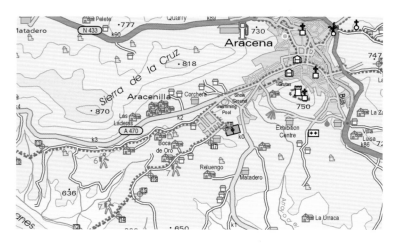

a steady uphill through the tree-dotted pastures to pass a *cortijo* before reaching a junction (Wp.12 65M) where a well stabilised track goes off to our right. *PR* waymarking confirms our route for us to come over a crest to pass a waypost, and at last we have easy strolling on a gentle descent through corked oaks, roughly parallel to the A470 road. We come down to a large Canarian pine (unusual in this region) outside a farmhouse (Wp.13) south of our track.

Our track, which was quite narrow at barely vehicle width, widens at a field entrance as we stroll along above cultivated plots to pass a *cortijo* (Wp.14) on our right. After a second *cortijo* we face an uphill section and start to catch glimpses of **Aracena** in the distance ahead. The grand houses of **Aracenilla** are visible to the north, as **Aracena**'s new urban housing comes into view ahead. We pass an old house on our left to come onto the new housing development by an 'Aracena - Linares de la Sierra' signboard (Wp.15 90M).

Leaving the countryside behind, we stroll along the street to meet the A470 road outside the municipal swimming pool **Piscina Municipal de Aracena** (Wp.16) to head across the road junction, walking against the traffic flow, to come to the first refreshment opportunity at **Bar/Restaurant Camino Real** (Wp.17 100M). If you can resist stopping here, then more bars are available as we pass the **Gruta de las Maravillas** parking area and walk uphill, and swing left to finish in the central **Plaza del Marqués de Aracena** (120m).

Linares de la Sierra is a focal point for walking routes, and here we have our southern approach to **Aracena**. Starting on well-used tracks, we then ascend an interesting valley on a little-used trail before coming back onto good tracks that lead us to the town's western outskirts.

* in **Aracena**

Access by Car
Park on the access road to **Linares de la Sierra** at the western end, by the street with the *fuente*.

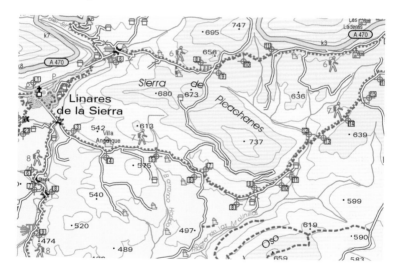

From the *fuente* (Wp1 0M), we head down the street to the T-junction where we can choose from two approaches; our PNF track shows us going right and then following the streets around to the cobbled street heading out of the town (SE) towards the river, while an alternative is to go left towards the church and work your way down the narrow streets to the cobbled street. For detailed directions see Walk 8, 'Linares de la Sierra River Route'.

Heading away from the town, we come down to the T-junction by the river (Wp.2 9M) where we go left to cross the little bridge and climb up the cobbled track between stone walls. Over the crest, the track changes to dirt until we come up to a cobbled bridge just before a T-junction (Wp.3). We go left to climb steadily up past rock outcrops, our track alternating between dirt, concrete and cobbling until we revert to dirt as the route levels out.

... signed 'La Molinilla' on a cork oak

We stroll past the entrance of **Villa Angelique** (Wp.4 19M) to a junction where we keep left to start climbing gently; on our left, the once proud villa is revealed to be a near ruin. We come over the crest, then stroll down to cross a *barranco* dropping steeply away on our right (Wp.5). Our easy track winds along between oak pastures, passing a track off to our left (Wp.6), our route ahead signed 'La Molinilla' on a cork oak above the junction. We continue until we meet a walking trail on our left (Wp.7 40M) marked by *PR* waymarks.

Here, we leave the track to take the walking trail as it follows a fence and is then enclosed by fences as we drop down and our trail widens to a track. Along the track we pass through a 'latch pin' gate (Wp.8) to curve left above a water-eroded gully before passing through the second 'latch pin' gate and onto a better track (Wp.9) coming up to us from the right (the extension of the track we were on earlier). Gently uphill (ENE), the track brings us up to a pair of substantial gates where it swings left (Wp.10) to go up to the old iron ore quarry of **Minas de Fatima**, while we go straight ahead on a narrower track signed 'PRA39 Aracena 3km' to come to the entrance gates (Wp.11) of the farm that occupies the valley floor.

Taking to a narrow trail beside the green metal gates, we climb above the farm through wild woodland (secateurs useful) before contouring along with the sound of running water rising up to us. Our trail drops down through the tangled shrubbery which finally gives way for us to meet a stream (Wp.12 65M). Hopping over the muddy crossing, we climb up a stony rock trail to a hairpin bend where our trail swings sharp left into a steady ascent along an eroded rock gully. The gradient eases, but we need to watch out for a narrow section (Wp.13) where rushing water has gouged out a 'rambler trap' in this otherwise comfortable trail.

We come up from the gully to overlook a tree-stuffed valley, the trees thinning towards a sloping *sierra* meadow as we gain height, until we come to a point where our onward trail is very overgrown (Wp.14 74M). From here it is easier for us to continue up the valley, crossing its watercourse before a stiff, puff and grunt ascent brings up onto a stony track at the head of the valley (Wp.15 80M).

The track runs over to a gated pasture as we go left past an old *PR* waymark, uphill until the stony surface gives way to comfortable dirt where we stroll between cork oak meadows to come to a junction (Wp.16 85M), where another track goes left. Keeping straight on, we go gently downhill to cross a ford, after which it's an easy uphill past **Villa Vasquez y Gonzalez**, an impressive pair of country residences. We have an easy uphill to pass the

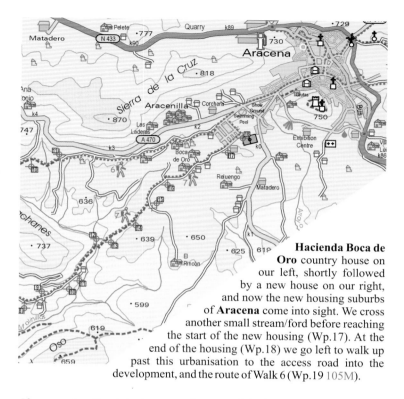

Hacienda Boca de Oro country house on our left, shortly followed by a new house on our right, and now the new housing suburbs of **Aracena** come into sight. We cross another small stream/ford before reaching the start of the new housing (Wp.17). At the end of the housing (Wp.18) we go left to walk up past this urbanisation to the access road into the development, and the route of Walk 6 (Wp.19 105M).

If you are heading into **Aracena**, then turn right (ENE) to walk along the access road and meet the main road at the entrance to the **Piscina Municipal de Aracena** (swimming pool) by the town´s western one-way system. Keep straight on (the traffic goes right) to walk against the occasional cars and past the local radio station to reach the square and junction below the **Gruta de las Maravillas**. To reach the main square, continue until you have the arts centre on your right and turn left at a supermarket opposite **Hotel Castaños**. At the end of the street turn right at the T-junction, to pass **Hotel Sierra de Aracena** and the famous **Jamones la Joya** shop before arriving at the corner of the main square (120M); **Bar Manzano** is a few steps away on your left, surprisingly the only bar fronting onto the square.

Some times we just want to take life gently, enjoy beautiful countryside, marvel at the splendid wild flowers and observe the wild life - a time when tranquility and beauty take precedence over high energy hiking. Add in a couple of rivers, a stone-built (but forgotten) *mirador* overlooking a craggy *barranco*, easy strolling on a comfortable track and a finish at an old stone bridge and riverside meadows, and you have our Linares River Route; simply beautiful.

Unfortunately (inevitably) the gentle downhill on our outward route becomes steady uphill on our way back resulting in a 2/3 Walker rating.

*linear and return

Access by Car

Park on the access road above **Linares de la Sierra**. Technically, you can drive to the river - but why you should want to is beyond us, and it involves working your way through the nightmare maze of streets that make up this small town; stick to your feet and relax.

> **Short Walk Option**.
> Basically as far as you like and return; the stepped stream access at Wp.7 22M, the bridge over the **Ribeira La Molinilla** Wp.8 27M, or the *mirador* rest area Wp.9 35M.

We start from the western end of the access road for **Linares** at the first street down into the town (Wp.1 0M) by a *fuente*. Taking the street (S) we go left at the T-junction (our Alájar route goes right here) and follow the street round to the right. We keep heading downhill through the maze of streets - by far the most difficult navigation of the whole route - and our PNF (Personal Navigator Files) shows an alternative loop through the western streets that we recorded on our outward route.

Our objective is the cobbled street running down into the country opposite house Nº13 (Wp.2). Down the street, we pass a parking area (we should give a prize for any tourist who manages to get their hire car this far!) and a cobbled trail joining us from the left (Wp.3 7M); if you start from the eastern edge of **Linares** this is probably where you'll join our route.

Now that we are clear of the town, we have an easy stroll down between cultivated plots to a T-junction beside a stream and a bridge (Wp.4; our Linares-Aracena route goes left here) where we go right to follow a cobbled track along the right bank of the stream. We pass a picnic area set beneath shady trees (Wp.5) and a steep concrete track climbs to our right; this is a dead end and not a way back to **Linares**! Our track changes to dirt as it climbs up to pass a house on our left before running gently downhill to cross a water runoff, after which our track undulates along, passing the entrances to orchards on our left.

Just as we think it's getting truly rural, we come to the unusual sight of a huge array of solar panels set in a meadow on our right (Wp.6) opposite the entrance to **AMR**. After that surreal sight, our track curves over a small bridge, just after which is a stone-stepped descent to the stream (Wp.7 22M); this is easily missed unless you step off the track, and is well worth the tiny diversion, especially if the interesting thirty centimetre snake we saw is still there.

Snake spotting at 22 minutes into the route

Back on the track, we stroll past a track off to the right to come to a bridge over the **Ribeira La Molinilla** (Wp.8 27M), and a waterfall set amongst the trees, after which it is uphill over a crest before coming back to easy strolling. Stone walls cut out the views for a short section until we pass an entrance and cross two concreted water runoffs before reaching the entrance to **El Molinillo de Juan Marquéz** beside a stone built *mirador* rest area (Wp.9 35M). Its table and benches appear little used which is surprising, given its tranquil location overlooking the craggy *barranco* walls.

Leaving the *mirador*, we climb over a crest to open views over the river valley and to the *sierras* before we stroll down past floriferous meadows to a bridge over the river (Wp.10 45M).

The old mule train stone bridge

The track continues over the bridge to climb the southern side of the river valley but we go left to the old mule train stone bridge that was the track's original route. Here is peaceful tranquility, or you could wander amongst the riverside meadows; really more *arroyo* (stream) than river, but no less beautiful for that aquatic definition.

We return to **Linares de la Sierra** by the same route.

Starting from stylish **Alájar**, following country paths to the once abandoned hamlet of **Los Madroñeros** (now being repopulated) and then on to **Linares de la Sierra**; beautiful countryside and only a couple of short 'puff and grunt' ascents would mark this out as a favourite walk, except for one poor section. Midway between **Los Madroñeros** and **Linares de la Sierra,** the once crystal clear stream of the **Barranco de los Madroñeros** is now a noisome flow of effluent from a big pig breeding farm, and across the stream the way is cut through briars for some distance and then followed by a kilometre of very piggy aroma. If you can tough your way through this difficult stretch, please take secateurs to keep the path open, then this is one of the most delightful routes you'll find in the whole Sierra de Aracena.

Access by car
Park on the western or eastern edge of **Alájar**.

Short Walk
A bit too energetic for a Stroll. Follow the alternative route out to Wp.7 and return by the traditional route, 30-40 minutes and a good appetizer before lunching in **Mesón El Corcho**.

Traditional Start
We start by parking on the eastern outskirts of **Alájar** by the signboard for the 'Alájar-Puerto de Linares-Linares de la Sierra' route of Walk 10 (Wp.1 0M) to stroll west on the main street, passing the start of **Arias Montano** street (Wp.2) and a *fuente* topped with a cross (Wp3) before coming to a small square, **Plaza del Baranquillo** (Wp.4). Following the sign for 'Centro Ciudad' takes us down to the end of **Virgen de la Salud** to face **Casa Padrino** (Wp.5) where we turn left to go down the cobbled street.

If you want to visit the centre of **Alájar**, then turn right at **Casa Padrino** to go past the church, and walk down past the **Caja de San Fernando** bank to come into the main square. (If you parked at the western outskirts, then walk down the main street until you pass **Mesón El Corcho** on your right and take the next street on the right. Check you are passing **Caja de San Fernand** to walk up past the front of the church and then down to **Casa Padrino**.)

We come down the street of **Pintor Antonio Milar** between traditional houses to cross the stream by a modern house in a *tipico* style, and then climb up towards semi-dilapidated houses (some being restored) to the remains of a signboard and a yellow and white *PR* waymark (Wp.6) on a cobbled track opposite a disused *ermita*. Swinging left (ESE), we start climbing the steep cobbled track. Cork oaks hang impossibly over the earth banks above us, as we labour up the mix of cobbling and concrete to come to a *PR* waymark and a log seat (Wp.7 16M).

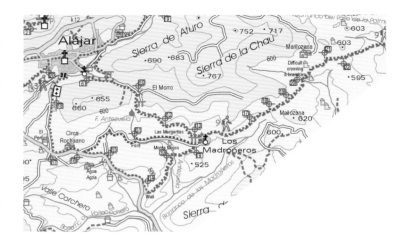

Alternative Start

That's the traditional route, but for the adventurous here is an alternative start. At **Arias Montano** (Wp.2) turn left down the cobbled street which will lead you down to a stream running in a concrete channel. Across the channel using the little steps, we come onto a dirt track where we go right, going steadily uphill and looking for the rough stone path which starts by a silver *agua* door set in the left hand bank. This rough path climbs steeply to bring us onto a comfortable dirt trail which curves left (S and then SE) above a farm and then runs along the steep side of a sharp valley - slightly vertiginous on one narrow section. As the valley's watercourse comes up to meet us our trail swings right to climb up a steep meadow, at the top of which we clamber through a gap in the stone wall to the log seat (Wp.7 12M).

Continuation

From the seat, a short rise takes us up to the track's crest (Wp.8) at the **Puerto de los Madroñeros** where the concrete ends, and that's the last we will see of climbing for some time as we continue on the stone and dirt track to pass a track off to our right (Wp.9). We are steadily descending, the track narrowing until, by a gated entrance (Wp.10), we have the unusual sight of concrete roads in the middle of nowhere - we are now definitely on a trail. Sections of the original cobbling are still intact as we cross a stepping stone ford near **El Moro** just before coming to another log seat facing the stone wall on our right (Wp.11); rather than take a break at this 'viewless' seat, hang on until the next one we come across.

Our trail is now dropping steadily with occasional stone steps and cobbled sections, but mostly it is stone-littered, requiring careful footwork to take us down to a waymarking post and *PR* paint (Wp.12 33M). Noisy 'herd' dogs assert their possession of the cork oak-studded sloping meadow on our right as we come down past **Cerca Las Margaritas** on a gate, just before our trail crosses a 'stepping stone and handrail' water run off. A gentle uphill section, then we contour round the hillside and the houses of **Los Madroñeros** come into view as we reach a perfectly positioned log seat (Wp.13 40M); now this is the place to take a break overlooking the beautiful valley, village and southern *sierras*.

From the seat we have a steep, stone-stepped descent down to a *fuente* (Wp.14), from where we curve up to walk between the houses; a path also leads down to a second *fuente* (S), to come up to the grassy square by the hamlet's church (Wp.15).

... the houses of Los Madroñeros come into view ...

Los Madroñeros once had a population of 150 people in the 19th century, dropping to zero towards the end of the 20th before being 'rescued' as an artists' colony and holiday homes. Several of the houses have recently been refurbished and modernised, electricity coming from solar power allowing some modern lighting. From our direction of approach, the settlement appears to have pedestrian access only, but south of the second *fuente* is a dirt track giving easy access for building materials, and it is perhaps only a matter of time before someone opens a bar and rural *hostal* in this idyllic location.

From the grassy square (Wp.15) we go up into the countryside onto a narrow trail which runs between the last houses by a *PR* waymark (Wp.16 NNE 50M). Our trail contours along through the tranquil countryside, crossing a couple of water runoffs and coming to a *PR* waymark (Wp.17 60M). Now we are climbing alongside a water runoff, cistus bushes pushing in on our route, to pass the gated entrance of **Marilozana**. Continuing up between stone walls we pass an open gate and *PR* waymark (Wp.18) to come to a second gated entrance to **Marilozana** (Wp.19 72M) at the crest of the trail.

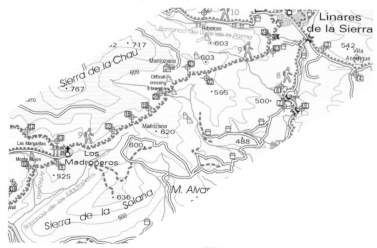

Now it is gently downhill between old stone walls colonised by abundant plant life, to approach the tall poplars marking the **Barranco de los Madroñeros** watercourse (Wp.20) and the most difficult section of the route. Crossing the noisome flow and boggy ground. we head up to a *PR* waymark on a stone wall. Our cobbled trail now heads into a briar tunnel - secateurs very useful - to struggle uphill through a second briar tunnel to emerge between pig paddocks.

It's very piggy as we walk up the stone-littered sandy trail to a *PR* waymark on a metal post (Wp.21 85M) where our route swings right (E) for us to leave the pigs behind as we pass an entrance to **Marilozana** (Wp.22). Now we are descending again, on deeply eroded rock before the route widens again and becomes a grassy path for easy strolling, as **Linares de la Sierra** is glimpsed ahead (NE) just as we are wondering where they had hidden the town.

We drop down between stone walls on the eroded trail to an old sign (Wp.23 106M) for 'Linares' ahead and 'Madroñeros' behind. A picky descent takes us down past iron gates and a lichen-covered stone wall to cross a tiny bridge (Wp.24) over a stream. We face a steep climb from the bridge up the overgrown cobbled trail until it clears by a gate, but the gradient continues as we come up to the first building and onto a cobbled street (Wp.25 117M). If you are planning to stop off in **Linares de la Sierra**, then head uphill through the maze of narrow streets to the church and its square, where steps lead you down to the unusual 'bullring' bar.

For those combining this route with Walk 10 for a circular route based on **Alájar**, we go left (NW) from Wp.25 on a pedestrian walkway to turn left (Wp.26) on a path which runs between walls topped with oranges. At a green gate on our left our path swings right (N) and climbs steadily alongside a water channel, and at the next junction we go right to climb up to the cobbled track of Walk 10 opposite the 'Linares - Alájar' signboard (Wp.27 112M).

In addition to it being an enjoyable route for those who like an uphill challenge crossing the **Puerto de Linares** at 700 metres altitude, this is a useful link for making circular walks with other routes calling at **Linares de la Sierra** and **Alájar**. Combine this route with Walk XX for a circular route based on **Alájar**, which has much better refreshment opportunities than the little that's available in **Linares**.

Access by car

If you are starting at **Linares de la Sierra**, then park at the western outskirts on the access road. Do not try driving on the streets of **Linares** unless you enjoy seriously high stress levels!

> **Stroll**
> Follow our route out to the picnic area beside the dammed lake in the **Barranco del Valle de la Palma** - 20 minutes each way, and a delightful picnic site.

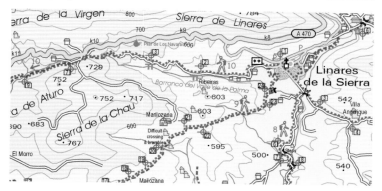

Our usual starting point is the 'Linares-Alájar' notice board on the cobbled trail out to the cemetery, as a link with Walk 9. To reach this point, take the first street down into **Linares**, easily identified by the *fuente* at the top. At the T-junction turn right for an easy stroll down the cobbled street to arrive by the signboard (Wp.1 0M).

From the signboard, we have an easy stroll away from **Linares**, passing the **Cementerio de Nuestra Señora del Carmen** where the cobbling changes to well-stabilised dirt track. We stroll past a newish large house before our track swings left (S) giving views back over the town. A water channel runs alongside the track as it swings right (W) and past three more newish large houses which lend an air of affluent suburbia. We come alongside a stream which plunges over a small waterfall as our track climbs gently through woodland and, over a crest, we cross a stepping-stone ford before climbing up past a dam to the **Riberas** recreation area (Wp.2 17M).

The Riberas recreation area

Two concrete tables and their benches are dotted on the grass meadow that runs down to the large pool created by the dam, while forest trees overhang the limpid water on the opposite bank. At weekends and *fiestas* this is a popular all-day picnic site for locals, but at other times you are likely to have this delightful setting to yourselves; make the most of this location in view of what is to come.

The track from **Riberas**, in poor condition, starts seriously climbing up through the hillside on this side of the *arroyo*. It becomes a slogging 'puff and grunt' ascent, taking breaks at the occasional pines, or when encountering a grazing horse or donkey - a log seat set below a pine makes a welcome break in the 200 metre ascent (Wp.3). The track gradually narrows and officially becomes a trail (Wp.4) as we come to the edge of woodland, and then climbs steeply through a pair of hairpin bends before a final slogging ascent through the trees brings us to a waymarking post on the **Puerto de Linares** alongside the tarmac road (Wp.5 58M).

The walking trail is signed over a hillock, and you'll probably feel like one if you obey the sign instead of taking the few steps on the tarmac to its other side and a multi-coloured waypost (Wp.6). A track runs ahead round the hillside, while we go right (WSW) on a steep track dropping down through the trees; possibly over-steep given its gritty surface and jittery muscles from the climb, so take care. At a gate entrance with 'Privado' stuck on a tree (Wp.7), **Alájar** is signed along a trail which runs along above the house served by the track (Wp.8).

Past the house, our trail winds steadily down through the greenwood accompanied by a stream on our right, which we cross with the assistance of steeping stones and handrail (Wp.9), to continue down the right bank. Our trail undulates along through the woods, widening at gate entrances (Wp.10) to descend more steeply on a concrete section before flattening out. We pass a couple of waypoints before a gentle climb brings us up to the 'Alájar-Linares' signboard alongside the access road on the eastern outskirts of **Alájar** (Wp.11 80M). From here it's a simple stroll into the centre of this little town to enjoy the excellent food and amazing decor at **Mesón El Corcho**, or in one of the bars for something simpler.

There's a beautiful country path from **Alájar** which climbs through chestnut groves to excellent views before descending to **Castaño del Robledo**. Right at the start we have the opportunity to see at close quarters the once-abandoned hamlet of **El Calabacino** which has been repopulated as a thriving artists' colony - mostly English artists from the home counties it seems. Generally, we are on well made paths and tracks, especially the descent into **Castaño del Robledo**, though one section of the climb is very badly water eroded; not dangerous, just uncomfortable.

Access by Car
Park on the western end of the **Alájar** access road from the A470.

Short Walk Option
To **El Calabacino** and return. 2 Walker. Twenty minutes each way.

From the western outskirts of **Alájar** (Wp.1 0M) we walk up the access road to cross straight over the A470 road onto a track, signed to **El Calabacino**, to climb steadily beneath large oaks to a gated field entrance (Wp.2) where our track continues ascending to the right. As we gain height the views increase over the beautiful valleys to the south. Passing the first cottage, our track is stone walled and we lose the views for a while, but notice the first of the quirky colourful signs that the colony is famous for; a request for people to leave their cars down below.

We cross a stream on a brick bridge (Wp.3 10M) beside a *lavadero*, our path narrowing to trail width as we climb above sloping meadows to a junction (Wp.4) beside a ruin. We keep right - the left hand path is signed 'El Calabacin' - to climb up below a grand building, where a path with a yellow dot goes right while we keep ahead to climb up around the building - now clearly a church from this viewpoint. It's a steady ascent through the trees on the cobbled trail to pass a cottage on our left, keeping to the main trail as it zigzags up the slope to a cork oak (Wp.5 18M) with a 'robin' and 'Basuras no Amigo' (No rubbish, friend) sign on its trunk.

Our cobbled trail continues climbing to a crest and then reverts to a dirt surface for us to pass a cobbled path down to a cottage before coming up to a junction (Wp.6 23M) where an 'El Castaño' artistic sign directs us up the narrower trail climbing to the right. We pass below the last lonely house in its isolated location to continue climbing between an earth bank and a stone wall, briars overhanging our narrow trail making secateurs a useful accessory until we emerge from this green tunnel (Wp.7 28M).

Now it is steeply uphill, plants pushing in on our narrow trail, before the gradient moderates and the plants relent to create a pleasant woodland path that crosses a water runoff and continues in a steady climb through the trees, re-crossing the water runoff to where orange and white incident tape (yes, incident tape) direct us up a narrow path through the undergrowth. Secateurs

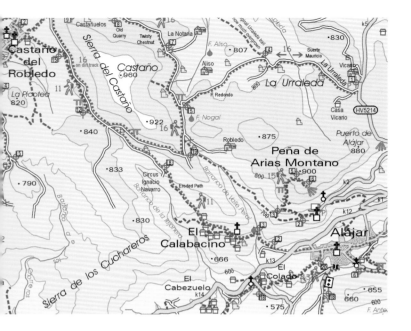

are useful to deal with intrusive plants as we push up the new path, the original path having gone up the water runoff but this is now too badly eroded to be passable for a section.

We come back to the line of the original path (Wp.8 33M), our route once a cobbled donkey trail, though now a washed out water runoff. We come up to a field entrance that caused the erosion, the trail beyond it in slightly better condition as we come up to a crest (Wp.9) - but unfortunately it's a 'false crest' as our trail swings right and continues climbing; again, badly water eroded until we step out onto the edge of a sloping meadow (Wp.10 40M) dotted with chestnuts and cork oaks.

Now that we've emerged from the forested slopes, our route takes on a more open aspect as we walk along the bottom of the meadow to pass the entrance gates to **Circus Ignacio Navarro** where we come onto a dirt track. It is still uphill through the chestnut groves, occasionally steeply, to pass below a brown stone hut before coming to a crossroads (Wp.11 54M) to join our **La Urraleda - Castaño del Robledo** route in reverse. From the crossroads we continue up the steady slope (NW) to finally reach a crest - a true crest this time (833 metres).

Now it is distinctly downhill with glimpses through the trees of the houses of **Castaño del Robledo** in the distance as we come down to a cairn (Wp.12 60M) that marks a walking trail diverging from the track. Taking the trail, we are dropping down in a gentle descent through vegetation which restricts the views, our trail paralleling the track (see La Urraleda-Castaño route for walking along the track). Red and white incident tape (used as a *GR* waymark) and a waypost, confirm our route as we come along to a second post and a log seat (Wp.13). Our woodland trail, shady on hot days compared to the track, continues with waypostrs at gaps which link to the track.

At a faint junction (Wp.14 68M) 'Castaño' is signed ahead on a rock beside the path as we come onto the track for thirty metres, red and white incident tape marking our path's continuation amongst the woodland. A section of gentle uphill is followed by gentle downhill to bring us to a waypost (Wp.15 72M) where our trail finally turns away from the dirt track to head down to **Castaño del Robledo**.

We descend a semi-stepped cobbled trail beneath a magnificent avenue of mature cork oaks, the scale of both trail and trees beyond anything seen on our route so far. The cobbled trail, more boulder-laid in nature, improves as we drop down but requires careful footwork in wet weather on its potentially slippery surface. Houses, closer this time, are glimpsed through the trees as we descend steadily from the trees to walk past a house wall and a signboard 'Rodeo Al Cerro del Castaño' and come onto a steep cobbled street (Wp.16 84M). Skittering down the steep street, **Calle Arias Montano**, we arrive in the tiny square beside the church to choose between **Bar la Bodeguita** and **Bar Nico** for refreshments (Wp.17 85M).

Bar Bodeguita at the end of the route

Walks in the Sierra de Aracena often bring us in close contact with the woodland, but this route is unusual for its very openness, even though it crosses forested slopes. Difficult to explain, but easy to recognise when you are on route. Even the towns have a different atmosphere, as we compare the expansiveness of **Castaño del Robledo** to the quiet, inward-looking **Santa Ana la Real** - or perhaps this is just our imagination.

This route is popular with locals on Sundays as they enjoy a contemplative stroll along the track after visiting the cemetery, when Land Rover drivers (!) are severely frowned upon; now, how would we know that? And no, the route is not driveable as you'll clearly see.

Access by Car
Turn off the H7015 at the southern entrance to **Castaño del Robledo** and park near the road to the cemetery, or if you wish to reduce the climb, then drive up to and park at the cemetery. On no account should you attempt to drive to our 'official' start point in the square by the church!

From the square (Wp.1 0M) we head down past the church on a stepped street. Our object in this maze of streets is go WSW to the lower, and larger, square (Wp.2) where **Dr. Tomás Muniz Pablos** (Bishop of Pamplona) is celebrated, and follow the **Calla Santa Ana** past the town sign to the 'melting ruins' at the start of the cemetery road by the signboard 'Castaño del Robledo - Fuente de los Casares. 1 Hour. Low Difficulty' (Wp.3 8M).

The steep climb up to the cemetery can be relieved by studying the disadvantages of mud construction, as evidenced by the 'melting ruins', before passing the *ermita*. At the cemetery, the concrete lane continues as a dirt track, climbing even more steeply after rounding the cemetery before levelling out at a *PR* waymark (Wp.4 16M). After that climb we get our reward in the form of a broad, well stabilised track for us to saunter along past chestnut meadows - no chance of getting lost, and our route confirmed by wayposts and *PR* waymarks, as we head gently downhill.

After a concrete section we have a gentle rise between earth banks, followed by a descent to another concreted section. The route then runs out to a waypost marking a junction with a minor track to our front left (Wp.5 25M). Now our track's surface changes to sand, to take us down above a tiny cottage (Wp.6) set amongst the woods, easily missed while we are heading downhill. We ignore minor logging tracks before swinging right in front of green gates (Wp.7 31M), where there's an old sign 'Robledo Santa Ana la Real' with the instructions to 'follow the electricity line'. Rather than cut across country following the pylons, we continue down the comfortable track through open scrubland to cross a water runoff.

Our gentle descent comes back amongst the trees, our track now eroded as we come into a steeper landscape to drop down past a pair of large holes (Wp.8 43M) and a logging trail off to our left. The rough track drops down through a hairpin bend, now so eroded as to make the *PR* waymarked trail (Wp.9) down a gully alongside a fence a viable option to skittering down the track.

... we come into a steeper landscape ...

Back on what remains of the track, by either option, we come down to join a track by a sign for 'Los Chorros' (Wp.10) to our right (NW). Now we are back to gentle strolling as we head down the track (SW) to a stream crossing on a pedestrian bridge alongside a ford (Wp.11 55M).

Easy finish

We are easily seduced into following the picturesque river valley on the track running beside the watercourse. Over another ford and bridge (Wp.12) we follow the left bank to pass the entrance to **La Hoyuela** and emerge onto the A470 road beside the 'Santa Ana la Real' signboard (Wp.13 62M). Now it is along the A470 to pass a water canal (disused) that crosses under the road, and a track signed 'no parking' on our left before we arrive at the **La Presa** junction (Wp.14 76M), opposite the cobbled donkey trail of our 'Energetic finish'.

Energetic finish

From the stream crossing on the pedestrian bridge (Wp.11) we look to go right, picking up a path (W) alongside green fence posts to start climbing through chestnut groves, the gradient increasing as our trail changes to stone for a steep ascent up to a junction beside a stone wall (E1). Going left, we continue climbing alongside the wall and keeping straight ahead when the wall ends.

Across the meadow, we come back onto a traditional trail that ascends gently alongside another wall. We go over a crest, then our trail narrows and descends as we push through the *retema* to come to a water runoff and junction (E2). Going left, we are climbing what was once a boulder-laid trail though now much eroded, in a picky and relentless ascent to come over the crest to a field entrance (E3). Dropping down between pines and chestnuts on the erosion-damaged trail, we come down to the A470 at the **La Presa** junction (Wp.14 76M).

We come down into the hamlet of **La Presa**, following *PR* waymarking along the narrow streets and onto a trail between stone walls to come down to a concrete bridge crossing a stream. We curve up from the stream, passing a smelly cowshed as quickly as possible, to a junction (Wp.15 82M) with signs for 'Alajar, Linares' left, 'Santa Ana' right and 'PRA38 La Presa, El Castaño' back the way we have come.

Our cobbled trail has widened to a cobbled road for us to ascend steadily to the impressive **Santa Ana** *fuente* and *lavadero* (Wp.16) at the edge of the town. Heading up **Calle Constitución** and then **Calle Antonio Diaz**, we have a stiff climb up between the houses towards the sign for the tempting if basic **Bar Quatro Esquinas**. Saving the bar for later, our climb tops out at the town square of **Plaza d'España** (Wp.17 90M), with its shop and *ayuntamiento* cowering beneath the bulk of the baroque church which dominates the town. **Santa Ana** has a distinct shortage of hostelries, so it's back to **Bar Quatro Esquinas**, where if the table (singular) and chairs are occupied, we'll take our refreshment standing at the bar.

13 SANTA ANA LA REAL - ALÁJAR

For fans of trees and meadows, this is the 'must walk' route of the Sierra de Aracena. Centuries ago this region was cleared of scrubland to make way for the 'industrial engine' of cork oak and pasture which, unlike the relatively short lived water mills economy, remains an economic force to this day. Here we find the oldest oaks set amongst a timeless valley landscape giving us the sensation that we are walking back in time, until we arrive in **Alájar** with its 'temple to cork', **Mesón El Corcho**.

If you've even half a mind to believe in time travel, then this walk from the 'dark' inward looking **Santa Ana la Real** through a timeless landscape to the 'light' of **Alájar** is an almost mystical experience that might convince you. On a less mystical level, but related here as an example of the dark side of **Santa Ana la Real** ; even as recently as 2002, a referendum was held in **Santa Ana** as to whether women should be allowed as deputies on the local council; the motion was voted down by 231 votes to 130 votes, 'dark ages' in deed and word.

There are plenty of tracks and trails criss-crossing these wooded pastures, so take careful note of our walk directions. For compass users the general rule is to keep heading roughly east. If you have a GPS loaded with our waypoints, or our PNF file, then wayfinding is a doddle - as usual.

Access by Car
Santa Ana isn't the easiest of the valley towns for parking, so pull off the A470 and park as close to the 'main' road as is feasible and walk in to the square beside the church.

We start out from the town square beneath the brooding church (Wp.1 0M) to head down **Calle Antonio Diaz** (NE) past **Bar Quatro Esquinas** to turn right onto **Calle Constitución** to come to the impressive *fuente* and *lavadero* (Wp.2 4M) and head out of town down the broad cobbled road to the **La Presa** junction (Wp.3 7M).

The main cobbled way curves left towards the hamlet of **La Presa** while we keep straight ahead (E) on a woodland donkey trail that runs between pig pastures beneath the mature cork oaks. We come down towards a water course, a dirt track going off to our left (N) to **La Presa**, and a water channel runs alongside our broad trail, changing from right to left before running away over the rocks. Our route is gently downhill, occasionally cobbled, to pass an isolated house (Wp.4 16M) after which our trail gets narrower and rougher.

Our route, despite the rough trail, is a gentle downhill stroll between cork oaks and meadows to pass a stone walled path (Wp.5) off to our left, *PR* waymarking confirming our path. We cross a water runoff, after which our path is much smoother. Water canals run along walls and across the meadows, one feeding a redundant water tank beside the path shortly before we pass the

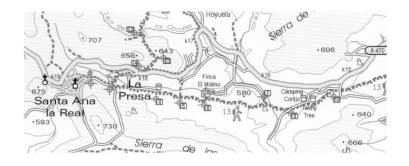

entrance to **Finca El Molino** (Wp.6 26M), the house itself hidden behind a high stone wall on the north of our track. From the *finca* it is uphill to a crest with a strange cave structure, out track narrowing to trail width for us to pick our way down the eroded stony gully. Just when we think it can get no rougher, it gets rougher before we arrive at gate entrances beside farm buildings (Wp.7 39M).

The twisty tree at 52 minutes.

A green track goes left from the buildings while we continue on the heavily-eroded trail to cross a ford - careful footwork needed on the stones, or simply wade through the mid-calf deep water. Now it's uphill on the comfortable grassy trail, confirmed by *PR* waymarking, and then down to another stream crossing before coming onto a dirt track (Wp.8 49M). Going left, we follow the rough track (ENE) up to a new house set amongst the woods opposite a very 'twisty' tree (Wp.9 52M). Following the fenced edge of the property, we pass below a second house before our trail brings us up to join a dirt track (Wp.10 59M) running below the A470 road; note the access tunnel under the road.

Heading east along the track, we come to a T-junction of tracks where we keep heading east on an eroded trail to come onto another dirt track (Wp.11). The comfortable walking surface doesn't last long as our route becomes water eroded, and the detritus from fallen walls add to the obstacles we must negotiate, including a fallen oak that we duck under. Our route smooths out after a gully takes the runoff away from our trail.

We drop down to cross a small ford, and then swing up to an old farm set in the fork of dirt tracks and trails (Wp.12 74M); the houses glimpsed beyond the farm are the hamlet of **El Cabezuelo**, not **Alájar**! A white arrow, and *PR* waymarking, direct us along a stone walled walking trail which runs steadily downhill (SE) between walled pastures to pass through cattle gates and to a T-junction of trails (Wp.13 81M) where we go left (E) and down towards the sounds of running water. An easy stream crossing brings us up to a junction (Wp.14) where we go left (E) up a rubble covered gully to another T-junction (Wp.15) where we again go left (N) following *PR* waymarking.

It is steady climbing up to a crest before continuing uphill on the trail, passing a waterfall drop on our left where storm waters leave the trail. We climb up the remains of a donkey trail to come below an industrial farm building, before a short steep climb brings us onto the access track outside the farm gates (Wp.16 96M).

We take the walking trail running alongside a deep water course, its surface becoming stone littered as we climb up to a tarmac road (Wp.17 100M) to go right and then left (Wp.18) onto a profusely waymarked trail signed to 'La Encina'; 'El Collado' is on our left. Our cobbled trail runs down to cross a stream on a little bridge (Wp.19) to then climb up past a farmhouse on our right.

Eventually the first buildings and the church spire of **Alájar** come into sight tantalisingly close, as we negotiate the rough trail to come to the first house (Wp.20 109M). Thankfully, our trail turns into a more comfortable street for us to come up to the main street where we turn right and stroll down past the **Hotel La Posada** to the amazing **Mesón El Corcho** facing the **Plaza d'España** (115M) and a choice of bars for refreshments.

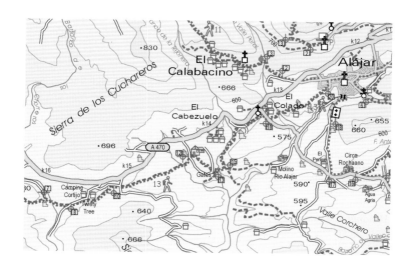

Los Madroñeros holds a special place in our affections because, besides being an extremely picturesque hamlet, it typifies the optimism of the artist over the pragmatism of mere mortals. From a state of unpopulated abandonment, **Los Madroñeros** is gradually reinventing itself as a thriving community despite its obvious isolation.

Here, we've contrived a route specifically to take in the hamlet and the beautiful scenery of the **Barranco de la Antezuela**, one of the least visited but most spectacular parts of the region, and there is a path to follow. Our whole route curves around the **Sierra del Camposanto**, but if you want to cut out the main ascents and descents we have a shorter circular route on the southern side of the *sierra*.

Access by Car
Park at the western outskirts of **Alájar** where there's plenty of on-street parking.

Short Walk Option
Park near the start of the **Los Madroñeros** dirt track, and follow the track (Wp.S1 a slippery ford, & Wp.S2 Circa las Margaritas/Monte Mojón) to the junction with our walking trail (Wp.9). From here you can walk up to explore the hamlet (Wp.8). Then follow our main route down the **Barranco de la Antezuela** and up the tarmac road back to your car. (3 Walker)

Alternative start from the east
From the eastern outskirts, walk in to **Arias Montano** street (Alt.1) to go left down the cobbled way to cross a concreted watercourse with steps, onto a dirt track (Alt.2) and turn right up to a trail (Alt.3) by a 'Contador de Agua' silver box set in the wall. Taking the steep trail walk up to curve around the hillside above a farmhouse and follow a sharp valley (possibly vertiginous). When the water course comes up to meet the path (Alt.4) our trail crosses the stream and climbs up across a sloping meadow to a gap in the stone wall where we join the main route beside the log seat (Alt.5).

Standard start
Starting on the western access road (Wp.1 0M), we walk down the main street between the imposing houses. After passing the square on our left and **Mesón El Corcho** on our right, we turn right onto **San Bartolomé** street (Wp.2) to pass the **San Fernando** bank and then go left at the church (Wp.3). We come down to pass **Casa Padrino** (Wp.4); now we are on our Walk 9 Alájar-Los Madroñeros-Linares route, so we'll keep description to a minimum.

Down **Pintur Antonio**, we cross the stream and climb up to the start of the **Los Madroñeros** trail (Wp.5) on **Concepción** street, for the ascent to the **Puerto de Los Madroñeros** pass (Wp.6 15M). Keeping to the main trail brings us down to the beautifully located seat above the village (Wp.7 35M); just the perfect place if you want to take a break.

... the second *fuente* ...

Down the steep trail to the edge of the hamlet, this time we keep **Los Madroñeros** on our left as we follow a small path down to the second *fuente* (Wp.8 40M) where we come onto the dirt access track serving the settlement. Along the narrow track, it widens to a small parking area where it crosses a water runoff (Wp.9). At this point a narrow trail runs down alongside the runoff - easily missed if you're not looking for it.

Taking the trail (SSW), we are strolling beneath mature trees flanked by a variety of daisies as the trail criss-crosses the runoff before bringing us to a stream crossing (Wp.10 48M). Across the stream, our trail climbs up to a stone wall, the sharp sided **Barranco de la Antezuela** opening up on our left. When the wall finishes a fence protects us from the steep drops. The abundant plant growth has narrowed our trail to a way, as we push through wild irises, daisies and an Agave americana where the fencing ends (Wp.11).

Passing the remains of an old 'fence' gate (Wp.12 53M), we continue pushing through clover and daisies as our way contours along the valley to follow the line of a low stone wall, before wandering away from the wall into woodland. Now our way disappears amongst the long grass beneath the shady trees. We walk across (E) to the corner of the stone wall (Wp.13 60M) that encloses the meadow in which we find ourselves. Clambering over the corner, we find a pile of rocks to assist our descent into a paddock alongside the tarmac road.

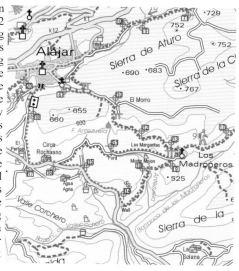

Heading (N) across the paddock, we come to a fenced corner where we can step through a gap to cross a water runoff and come onto the tarmac road (Wp.14). **Alájar** lies to the north of us behind the **Sierra del Camposanto**

Abundant plant life on this route

(which rises to 660 metres) and having had a lot of downhill, we know what to expect. Turning our faces to the north, we head up the tarmac road overlooking the **Barranco de Aquafría**, tarmac is replaced by concrete on a steeper section; a section of armco crash barrier doubles as a seat for a break in our ascent. Onwards and upwards, we come to the **Agua Agria** entrance gates (Wp.15) and the gradient eases for an easier stroll up to the **Los Madroñeros** dirt track (Wp.16 82M), signed to 'Virgin de la Salud' and 'Los Madroñeros', the start/finish of our Short Walk option.

It's still steadily uphill past **Circa Rachaano** to the crossroads (Wp.17 88M) and pass of **Puerto de las Erillas** where we leave the tarmac on a dirt track (N) which heads gently up past the back of **El Perijón** before dropping down across a ford to a junction (Wp.18), where another track goes left and back to the tarmac road.

Now our gentle strolling beneath the trees turns into an ascent, bringing us up past a large barn to an unnamed pass (Wp.19 97M) and views over **Alájar** to **Peña de Arias Montano**; a track goes back from our route to the tarmac road. An easy stroll brings us down to the cemetery, and the track becomes concrete surfaced and then traditionally cobbled for us to stroll down to an *ermita* at the edge of **Alájar** (Wp.20). We cross an old stone bridge and come into the maze of town streets to head uphill on **San Antonio**, going left at its end and keeping uphill on **San Bartolomé** to pass the church (Wp.21 110M) and drop down into **Alájar**'s main square to seek out refreshments.

Arias Montano was advisor to the Spanish king who retired to the wild border lands to contemplate the major events of those days. It is said that he would climb up to the high seat of the mountain that is now named after him, to look out over the distant lands for signs of inspiration as to what action he should advise the king to take.

We can repeat Arias' climb, though whether we will gain any insight into solving the world's problems is speculative, but at least we can enjoy a really good view for our effort.

| 3 | 1 H | 2½ km | 174m / 174m | * | 2 |

* and return

Access by Car
Drive up the HV5214 **Alájar-Fuenteheridos** road and turn into the **Peña de Arias Montano** entrance to its car park, then walk up to the **Ermita de Nuestra Señora de los Angeles** - technically an *ermita* but in our opinion, easily grand enough to be called a church.

Views over Alájar from Peña de Arias Montano

From the *ermita* and the bars, shops and no so cheery nut sellers (Wp.1 0M) we head west across the meadow on a walking trail to the 'Sierra de la Peña' signboard (Wp.2); '717 metres, 20 minutes, medium difficulty' though we rate the walk as longer than this. Even at only this short distance from the *ermita* we have left 99% of the visitors behind, as we head up the trail in a steady ascent (WNW) and climb up through a zigzag (Wp.3).

Now our general direction is north, and it's all uphill on one of the steepest trails in the region; the views that open up south over **Alájar** can be enjoyed while getting our breath back. We climb above the tree line and continue to ascend through low scrub, reaching the welcome sight of a stone seat (Wp.4) on a gentler section of the climb. Above the seat, we stay on the main trail as it curves up to our right (E) and a rock outcrop (Wp.5) can double as another 'seat' rest point. Coming up to a gentle crest (889 metres) it comes as a surprise to see that we actually need to go <u>down</u> to the *mirador* (Wp.6 25M 883 metres).

A signboard at the *mirador* explains the view that faces us, and the stone seat makes a fine picnic spot in good weather. Whether Arias Montano found inspiration at this point is not recorded, and it anybody's guess that he possibly just came up here for the spectacular views as a contrast to spending his days deep down in the steep valleys.

This is a delightful country strolling route amongst the chestnut meadows east of **Castaño del Robledo** without any major ascents/descents except down the steep streets to the town square for refreshment. In addition to the usual excellent range of flora, wild peonies favour the presence of the chestnut trees of this region.

La Urraleda is a well known (locally) country track favoured for Spanish family strolls, but it goes from nowhere to nowhere so we've combined it with a little-known route down into **Castaño del Robledo** and a section of our **Alájar** route, to create a pan-handle circular. The steepest parts of the route are the street descent to the little bars in **Castaño**'s tiny square and the ascent back to rejoin our route.

2/3 | 3 H | 9½ km | 230m / 230m | ⟳ | 1

Access by car
On the **Alájar** road, south of **Fuenteheridos**. Either turn into the lane where there is 'off track' parking, or park carefully alongside the tarmac road.

Short Walk
Omit the pan-handle and follow the circular route based on **Castaño del Robledo**.

We start out from the 'La Urraleda' signboard (Wp.1 0M) to stroll along the track and then go right at a track junction (Wp.2) where a waypost points us through open gates alongside the off-track parking area.

Pollarded chestnuts, a few minutes into the route

It's easy strolling through the woods, spotting our first wild peony (Paeonia mascula) as we come into groves of pollarded chestnut trees. We go over a rise to stroll gently downhill between meadows of grazing sheep, dotted with ancient trees.

Past a ruin, views open up over the northern *sierras* as we go gently downhill past gate entrances, our route curving towards the wooded peak of **Castaño** (962 metres, and the highest point in the Sierra de Aracena) as we come to the centre of a shallow valley.

Now we have a gradual uphill to an old *cortijo* (Wp.3 17M) and a waypost before passing a gated track to an old ruin on our left. At an old *GR* waymarker (Wp.4 22M) the old 'official' **Sendero de la Urraleda** continued straight on at this point, but we keep on and up the comfortable main track which takes us over a crest and then down to cross the valley floor.

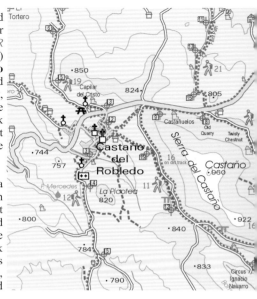

Once over a crest into a steeper valley, we see an old stone hut set amongst the chestnut groves ahead as we go down across the valley floor, the track splitting and rejoining as we come up to a junction, signboard, waypost and log seat (Wp.5 36M).

We are now at the end of the 'pan-handle', facing the choice of directions around **Castaño del Robledo**. On the Sierra de Castaños signboard, 'Sendero de la Urraleda' (new official route) goes right (NNE), and 'Sendero Rodeo Alsao Castaño' goes left (S).

Taking the **Sendero de la Urraleda** route, we head (NNE) along the track to pass below the stone hut (Wp.6), our track running steadily downhill to cross a stream. We ascend past a ruin as the track starts to curve around the hillside, bringing us to the gates of **La Notaria** (Wp.7 47M) and an interesting *cortijo* with a ceramic plaque to, 'Ignacio Navarro Erennis 1947' on the doors of the building. The dirt track is now immaculately stabilised, making for comfortable strolling up past a meadow packed with wild blue lupins as our route curves towards the west with views over the *sierras*. After contouring around the hill we start to drop down into a valley, our track lined by yellow broom and changing to concrete before it runs down to the **Castaño - Fuenteheridos** road by a waypost (Wp.8 58M).

Turning left, we head up the quiet road (W) past the entrance to **Castañuelos El Marqués**, until steps lead us up to a waypost set on a path above the road (Wp.9 63M). The trail runs along above the road to a track which runs into the chestnut groves. From the track we take a path alongside a stone wall marked by *PR* sign and a waypost (Wp.10); you could follow the track which runs into our return route (see map) but you would miss an exciting walking route and refreshments. Our trail becomes more defined as we drop down alongside the wall, pushing through vibrant shrubbery (secateurs useful), dropping into a steep gully beside the blood-red trunk of a corked oak. A slip-slide descent drops us into the bright green moss-covered gully where we carefully follow the stepped floor until suddenly we come into the open by a waypost.

Continuing down and ducking under a fallen tree we come out of the trees to water tanks at the top of **Castaño del Robledo** (Wp.11 79M). Now it's simply down the steep cobbled street, noting **Calle La Fuente** (Wp.12 and our onward route) as we skitter down the cobbles to the small square for refreshments at **Bar La Bodequita** or **Bar Nico** in **Plaza del Álamo** (Wp.13 82M).

After refreshment (0M) we face the steepest climb of the whole route - back up the steep cobbled street to **Calle La Fuente** (Wp.12) where we turn right (S) to leave the houses and come onto a cobbled trail by a signboard and waypost. Our trail climbs steadily up through the dappled shade of the mature trees that line our route, passing a track off to our left as stone steps bring us up to a waypost on the dirt path continuation of our trail (Wp.14 12M).

We use this path on our **Alájar-Castaño de la Robledo** route (Walk 11), but today we step up onto the dirt track which parallels the path (Wp.15). Our track contours along and then gently descends before coming up a 'puff and grunt' ascent to crest a rise (Wp.16 22M). Once over the rise we are back to easy strolling, passing glimpses of the walking trail, including a wooden seat (Wp.17), until it comes up to join our track (Wp.18 25M). Now both routes run down to a track crossroads and waypost (Wp19 30M).

Our **Alajar-Castaño** route (Walk 11) continues straight on down the valley, while we go left (E) to climb steadily, before our track starts to curve around the peak of **Castaño**, passing a *cortijo* (Wp.20). Now our track contours along above the steep valley with chestnut trees stalking the slopes, and there's a thoughtfully placed log seat (Wp.21 35M). There are terrific views over the southern *sierras* from our elevated track until we start climbing amongst pines. We come up to a waypost junction (Wp.22 43M) where a faint track runs off through the trees to our right (S). Keeping on the main track, we climb to a crest (851 metres) where the meadows become fenced, then have an easy stroll down past a waypost (Wp.23) and a gated entrance to a *cortijo* before coming back to the signboard and seat (Wp.5 50M), From here we have an easy walk back along the **La Urreleda** track to our car (Wp.1 85M).

This delightful route links the ham towns of **Jabugo** and **Galaroza** and returns by the **Ribeira de Jabugo**. An essential first route if staying at **Hotel Galaroza Sierra**. Wild flowers, which are excellent on our ascent to **Jabugo**, become exceptional on the descent of the river valley.

Access by car
Park in the square off the main road eastern entrance to **Galaroza** or along the wide street running away from the main road.

Extension
Exploring the ham town of **Jabugo**.

Technically, our route starts opposite the entrance to the **Galaroza Sierra Hotel** and to reach this point from your parking place, simply stroll down the main road with its 40 kilometre speed limit sign, to pass the 'Ribeira de Jabugo' path and sign board (our return route) and the **Hostal Venecia**, before coming to the walking trail opposite the hotel entrance.

Stepping onto the **Camino Galaroza - Jabugo** (Wp.1 0M) we walk down past a junction, where a private track goes up left, to come to a ford (Wp.2) which we cross on triangular stepping stones. Our track now climbs up to pass a new house (Wp.3 5M), and a track goes left as we continue ascending above

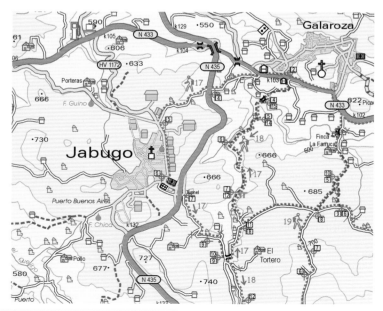

a semi-cultivated valley to pass a second house and a well used track, **Camino de al Questa del Vado**, going down to our right. Our track climbs up past a house, bringing the main road into view ahead. As we ascend to pass the entrance to **Luís Moreno Olivera** our track becomes tarmacked, to bring us onto the road (Wp.4 12M).

The track about 15 minutes into the route

Carefully crossing the main road, we come onto another track to head steadily up the cork oak studded slopes between white cistus. After a steeper section the track moderates as we pass a smallholding on our left before climbing again between stone walls. Passing a gated entrance on our right, we come up through the wooded slopes to the rear wall of a large ham factory, our track changing to concrete and then to tarmac, for us to step out to the **Jabugo** main street (Wp.5 25M).

Strolling up the street, we come to a choice of refreshment stops just past the **Oro Serrano** water fountain; we choose **Bar La Parada** (30M) for coffees and glasses of water. The main town of **Jabugo** is west of the main street, welcoming you to wander round its old square lined with 'leg of ham' shops that cater for the day tripper coach potatoes. The enthusiasm of the Jabugans for you to exchange money for a *jamón* knows few bounds, as almost everyone you meet implores you to buy the famous product.

To continue (0M) we stroll up the main street of **Carretera San Juan del Puerto** to its end at a junction facing the cemetery (Wp.6 3M) where we swing left to go down the pavement past a sports complex towards the main road. At the end of complex we go right to take the tunnel under the main road to face gated entrances and a narrow track (Wp.7 8M) signed 'Camino de Jabugo a Castaño del Robledo'.

Taking the track, we are immediately back in the countryside, contouring along and overlooking a valley, then descending as we start to pass pollarded chestnut trees. We drop down to cross a water runoff in the crook of a small valley (Wp.8), followed by a little uphill to pass an abandoned *cortijo* on our left (Wp.9) and then we are strolling gently downhill through yellow broom, pollarded chestnuts and pines towards the sounds of running water. A cottage marks the junction (Wp.10 22M) with our **Ribeira de Jabugo** route, a bundle of marker posts offering 'Castaño Bajo' straight ahead ,as we turn left around the cottage to cross a bridge over the stream.

Down the right hand bank, we pass through trees as the stream drops away on our left as we move away from the water to pass a restored cottage. After a second building we come to a track junction (Wp.11); our route is the 'Camino de Galaroza a Castaño del Robledo' while the 'Camino Castaño de Robledo a Fuenteheridos' goes right (ENE) offering a link to Walk 19. Keeping left, we pass another smallholding on our left where our route comes down to a walking trail width for us to push through green tunnels; secateurs useful. Our trail comes back towards the stream to overlook an almond grove and shortly after a waymarking post we come to a woodland seat (Wp.12 37M) an idyllic location to take a break overlooking the **Ribeira de Jabugo**.

The flora, which has been good so far, now becomes exceptional with classic specimens of woodland flowers lining our path as we follow the narrow trail above the steep river valley. Take care not to step off the path and note that some short stretches might just classify as vertiginous; follow our 'Look where you are walking, and stop to look at the view.', or more likely 'at the plants' on this trail.

We come out of the trees to pollarded chestnut trees stalking up the eastern slopes, our trail climbing a short slope before levelling out again. Now it is a gentle downhill stroll through a myriad of wild plant species (far too many to list here) that contrast with the main road's crash barrier glimpsed to the west. Passing the remains of a cottage (Wp.13) we have an easy stroll as we move away from the stream to pass above another almond grove meadow before turning above another crumbling building (Wp.14) set in the cleft of a side valley.

As we approach **Galaroza** the trail becomes boulder-walled for us to drop down a stepped green tunnel before glimpsing our first house. We come down to the sounds of rushing water and a 'Ribeira de Jabugo' signboard, just before a bridge over the stream.

Crossing the bridge

Crossing the bridge (Wp.15 60M), we climb up a cobbled donkey trail to come onto a dirt track which serves the house we glimpsed earlier. The track becomes cobbled to run over a crest, then narrowing to trail width beside a stone and brick wall before coming onto a cobbled trail (Wp.16) where the **Camino La Mimbreras** takes us past farm buildings to meet the main road (Wp.17 68M) beside the damaged *camino* posts and 'Ribeira de Jabugo' signboard. If you've parked at the eastern edge of the town, then go right to walk up to your car, or if starting from the **Hotel Galaroza Sierra** turn left, for the option of dropping into **Bar Venecia** before returning to our start point.

The **Ribeira de Jabugo** valley is one of the most floriferous places in all of the Sierra de Aracena, and while many of our routes are excellent for wild flowers, this route is truly exceptional. The ascents of the first hour simply melt away in the beautiful surroundings, though the final ascent into **Castaño del Robledo** is quite a gruelling climb.

Short Walk Option	**Short Circular walk Option**.
To the log seat at Wp.7 and return. (2/3 walker 1.25 hours)	Take the main route to track junction at Wp.8, then go east on the **Camino de Jabugo a Fuenteheridos** until Wp.9 of Walk 19 and then follow that route back to **Galaroza**. (3 walker 1.5 hours)

Access by Car
Park in the square off the main road eastern entrance to **Galaroza** or along the wide street running away from the main road.

From the square at the eastern entrance to **Galaroza** (Wp1 0m) we have to walk down the N433, with its 40 km speed limit, to the start of the official 'Ribeira de Jabugo' start at its signboard (Wp.2 6M) '6.7 kilometres, 2 hours, low difficulty' and a waypost for the 'Camino Galaroza a Castaño Bajo'; if you find yourself at **Hostal Venecia**, then you are just past the trail! Leaving the road behind we head south, keeping to the main cobbled trail at the **Camino de las Mimbreras** junction. Our trail narrows to walking width as it follows a stone wall, and then climbs up a gully to a crest; the views back over **Galaroza** are the last we will have for some time.

We descend to cross an old water canal (Wp.3 12M) before coming onto a dirt track which serves a house on our right; we cross over the track to drop steeply down into a wooded river valley where we cross the **Río Múrgia** on a cute but slightly vertiginous pedestrian bridge (Wp.4 15M) to a 'Ribeira de Jabugo' signboard.

A dank trail makes a steady ascent up from the bridge to come into the open, overhearing rather than overlooking the **Ribeira de Jabugo** as it runs noisily down its tree-lined water course. As this is a valley, we go gently uphill on the broad walking trail to head towards its source, passing above a roofless barn (Wp.5) as we stroll amongst the valley's trees and meadows to pass a second ruin.

As the river comes into view a faint path (Wp.6) leads down to the water, our trail and the river swinging left (from SW to S) for us to keep ascending between the green river valley and chestnut groves, an amazing variety of wild flowers lining our route in the dappled shade. The trail even runs gently downhill for a section before ascending again through this region of unspoilt

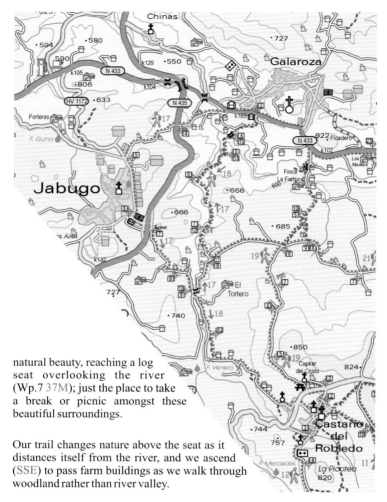

natural beauty, reaching a log seat overlooking the river (Wp.7 37M); just the place to take a break or picnic amongst these beautiful surroundings.

Our trail changes nature above the seat as it distances itself from the river, and we ascend (SSE) to pass farm buildings as we walk through woodland rather than river valley.

A briar-roofed green tunnel encloses us for a short time before we emerge to pass a gate entrance and building, where our trail widens to a driveable track taking us up past a smelly pig yard and to a junction marked by a profusion of *camino* waypoints (Wp.8 45M). Keeping right, our track goes past a couple of picturesque cottages before bringing us back alongside the river, where we stroll along beneath the tall trees to a concrete bridge (Wp.9 51M).

From the bridge, we climb up to a junction by a stone and tile house; here, Walk 17 comes down the track on the right to follow our route in reverse down to **Galaroza**. We turn left, following the track left at a junction with a 'Castaño del Robledo' signboard, and re-cross the river at a ford with stepping stones (Wp.10). Back on the right bank (geographically), we come up past **El Tortero** on the track, steadily climbing amongst the soaring trees.

Opposite a large house on the western bank (Wp.11 58M) our gentle ascent becomes a puff and grunt climb bringing us up to an elevated position above the river. Ascents are our constant companions during this second hour of the route, while elevation and enervation hold hands whenever we take a break in the climb. We continue uphill to a junction (Wp.12 62M) where we leave the track on a trail climbing up (S) amongst the chestnut meadows, to emerge onto a dirt track alongside a house, waypost and *GR* tape (Wp.13). We will stay on this track all the way to **Castaño Bajo** so we gird ourselves for the ascent without any wayfinding worries.

Looking towards Jabugo

Onwards and upwards, our trail becoming cobbled and concreted for the steeper slopes, **Jabugo** comes into sight on our right well before any sign of **Castaño del Robledo**, as our gradient finally eases from steep to moderate (Wp.14 80M) allowing a comfortable walking pace.

The river valley widens out to a great bowl of trees on our right as we stroll up past the outlying houses of **Castaño Bajo**, our concrete track reverting to dirt before we pass a walking trail and shrine (Wp.15) to come to the edge of the lower town.

We keep left, going gently downhill and then curving up to the right to come onto the H7015 road (Wp.16 90M) by the 'Bar La Bodeguita' and 'El Rincón de Pepe' signs. Straight over the road we head up into **Castaño del Robledo** to pass the unfinished second church (Wp.17) and *lavadero* (Wp.18) on our way up to the **Plaza del Álamo** (Wp.19 95M) beside the church and the choice of **Bar Nico**, **Bar La Bodeguita** and **El Rincón de Pepe** for refreshments.

If **Ribeira de Jabugo** has its flora, then this elevated route between the two towns should be famous for its views as we follow the 750 metre contour around **Picotea** peak before descending from the chestnut groves on easy track and trail. Just the route to blow away the cobwebs and take in the expansive views.

The most difficult aspect of this walk is finding the start. If in doubt, use the 'Access by Car' instruction.

Access by Car
Do not drive into **Castaño del Robledo**, but stay on the H7015 to pull into the small recreation area of **Capilar del Cristo** north of the town.

If you are starting from **Plaza del Álamo** in the centre of **Castaño del Robledo** (Wp.1 0M) then head uphill on **Talero** and turn left at its end (NNW). At the next T-junction we go right (NNE) on **Calle Fuenteheridos** (Wp.2) to climb away from the houses to meet the H7015 road (Wp.3) - that's the most energetic ascent of the whole route behind us.

We were tempted by the dirt track opposite, that runs downhill (NW) to a house where we go left, to drop down a very eroded trail through a green tunnel to emerge at the 'El Castañar' signboard and shrine. However, it is far easier to just walk down the tarmac road to the signed 'Capillar del Cristo' recreation area (Wp.4 10M) to join the car drivers; note our PNF takes the track and trail.

Capilar del Cristo is a tree-shaded haven on hot days where one can rest in the green dark beneath the leaf canopy; almost a timeless refuge hidden amongst the trees. From this refuge (0M), a dirt track leads past the signboard and shrine and takes us up a small rise before levelling out to a gentle up hill with the views opening up over the *sierras* as we top a crest (Wp.5 10M) and settle into a gentle downhill stroll (N).

Superb views over to **Cortegana** and its castle, **Galaroza** glimpsed ahead, and **Jabugo**'s hill top location all stand out as we pick our way along the stone-littered trail between chestnut groves to a junction (Wp.6 18M) with a gated entrance.

Our trail swings right over a small rise and then swings left, resuming its downhill nature through the chestnuts and yellow broom, the trail surface still eroded, then very eroded (Wp.7) just before we pass an old hut on our left. We pass a bare rock outcrop on our left just before a T-junction of tracks (Wp.8 32M); 'Castaño el Robledo' is signed back the way we have come, 'Camino de Jabugo a Fuenteheridos' is right (Walk 21), and left is a kilometre away

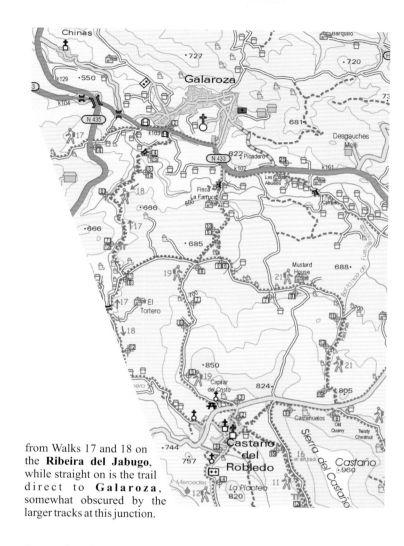

from Walks 17 and 18 on the **Ribeira del Jabugo**, while straight on is the trail direct to **Galaroza**, somewhat obscured by the larger tracks at this junction.

Our preferred route is to go right (E) on the **Camino de Jabugo a Fuenteheridos** and then take a narrow walking trail (Wp.9 39M), signed 'Camino del Puerto', which heads north through the trees and scrub to meet the main **Galaroza** trail (Wp.10 45M) at a 'Camino de Galaroza a Castaño del Robledo' waypost. This is our preferred route, but we have recently found both ends of this supposedly public path deliberately blocked by old branches, which we've cleared. If you don't find the path within our times, then return to Wp.9 and continue on the main **Galaroza** trail to Wp.10. We head down the eroded trail through a chestnut woodland (NE) displaying strong signs of storm water damage, before coming onto a boulder-laid surface with the **Ermita de Santa Brigida** standing out ahead of us.

Down past the rear of a house on our right, we carefully pick our way down the

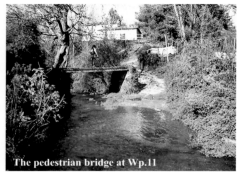
The pedestrian bridge at Wp.11

slippery boulder trail to pass the rear wall of a second house on our right, and a house entrance on our left. Now the trail becomes a driveable track accessing the houses, a noisy stream heading downhill alongside us as we pass more houses and entrances. We drop down to cross a swiftly flowing stream on a cute pedestrian bridge (Wp.11 58M).

Over the stream, it's uphill on the track, passing a 'Camino Particular' to come up to the N433 main road (Wp.12 63M) by the 'semaforo' speed limit lights. Turning left, we walk down the road to cross over to the square on the eastern entrance to **Galaroza** (Wp.13 67M), where a couple of utilitarian bars can offer refreshment.

The Sierra de Aracena is criss-crossed with *caminos* which form a network of connecting trails. The **Camino de Galaroza** is one such route, linking the two prosperous small towns of **Fuenteheridos** and **Galaroza**, as well as acting as a link into our network of walking routes.

Access by Car
Park either around the square in **Fuenteheridos**, on the access road from the N433, opposite the football ground, or in the signed parking areas, and then walk to **Plaza el Coso**.

Plaza Coso with its '12 pipes' *fuente* in the centre of **Fuenteheridos** is our start point (Wp.1 0M), which we leave by walking up the street from the north-west corner of the square. We could keep on this street up to the H7015 road and turn right to find the start of the **Camino de Galaroza**; however, our choice is the more scenic route, so we go right (Wp.2) to walk up the street to the T-junction at its end (Wp.3). Turning left, we leave the houses behind and climb up the cobbled street to the ghoulishly ornate cemetery (Wp.4), where the cobbles give way to dirt as the track takes us over a rise and down to the H7015, at the start of the **Camino de Galaroza** (Wp.5 7M).

We head down the dirt track, passing two trails off to our right and the access track (Wp.6) to **El Vey** as we stroll gently downhill through the quiet chestnut meadows dotted with wild flowers to a junction (Wp.7 15M) where we go down left, our track narrowing to a trail after the junction. We wind downhill alongside a plant and tree filled water course, our trail splitting either side of an old chestnut bole (Wp.8) and coming together again to run alongside the steep water course.

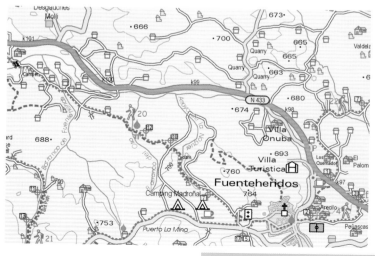

... the resting log ...

Surprisingly, the steep water course disappears - yes really - to be replaced by a shallow depression that our trail follows for a muddy section before reaching a stone barrage across the stream bed (Wp.9) at which point our trail curves away up into pine woods and to an old stone wall topped with fencing (Wp.10 26M) at a track junction. **Jabugo** is ahead as we cross the faint track and follow the line of the wall, dropping down into woodland again to come to the unlikely sign for **Barranco del Oso** (Wp.11 32M) placed high up on a chestnut bole. Our trail splits, and then meets up again, before we come to a 'resting log' set in a dappled shade glade beside the trail (Wp.12 37M); just the place to break the route amongst this soothing woodland, even more appropriate if climbing from **Galaroza**.

From the 'resting log' glade, our trail crosses a water runoff (difficult in wet weather) for us to stroll along to the hollow bole of a pollarded chestnut (Wp.13) beside our trail; a 'must' photo with your partner standing inside the tree.

After experiencing disappearing water courses, strange signs, a resting log and the 'Robin Hood' style hollow tree, we finally leave this enchanted woodland to come into a tamer landscape of fenced and farmed chestnuts, views opening up to the northern *sierras* as we pass a cottage on our right and come onto a broad dirt track at its entrance gates (Wp.14).

The Robin Hood tree

Now it is downhill (WNW), passing a gated entrance before coming to a waypost (Wp.15) signed for the 'Camino de Galaroza a Castaño Bajo' by a crossroads of tracks where we keep straight ahead (NW). We walk between shady earth banks and come down to a neatly lawned property signed 'Turismo Rural 959-501181' (Wp.16 52M) just before a 'Camino Viejo de Galaroza a Fuenteheridos' waypost at a junction.

We take the lower cobbled trail, going down to a ford and bridge (Wp.17). We follow the churning waters through deep woodland before a cobbled uphill takes us away from the stream and we reach a junction by a house (Wp.18).

Keeping right, we come down to pass a property entrance on our right, then a second entrance before passing an unusual 'country property' on our left

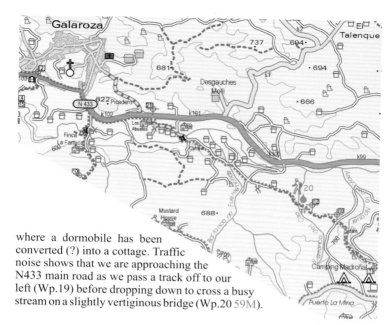

where a dormobile has been converted (?) into a cottage. Traffic noise shows that we are approaching the N433 main road as we pass a track off to our left (Wp.19) before dropping down to cross a busy stream on a slightly vertiginous bridge (Wp.20 59M).

Climbing up the cobbled trail from the bridge, we pass the **Posada de Alájar** to come to houses beside the track just before a junction where the **Camino del Torito** goes off to our right. After the houses we have an easy stroll down the track past the **Fuerta los Abjuelos** property before arriving at the N433 main road (Wp.21 67M). We are still a little distance from **Galaroza**, requiring an easy walk down the side of the main road, the traffic fast until drivers hit the 40 kilometre semaphore-controlled speed limit. Our **Camino de Fuenteheridos** (Wp.22) goes off to the south as we cross over to the main street into **Galaroza** for refreshments at **Bar Avenida** (Wp.23 80M) at the end of the square.

The **Camino de Jabugo a Fuenteheridos** was once one of the major transport routes in the region until the introduction of tarmac and motorised vehicles. It remains an interesting walking route on well stabilised tracks for much of its length, but the central section is almost forgotten, so expect to be alert to wayfinding when the track finishes; GPS comes into its own again on this 'forgotten' section. At the end of the forgotten section, we come onto the quiet H7015 road for two kilometres of road walking, not as dull as it sounds, before dropping into **Fuenteheridos** by its 'back door'.

Access by Car
Turn off the N433 into the eastern end of **Galaroza** and park on the square or the broad street leading off the square.

Short Walk Option
Take the track north from Wp.8 to the H7015 road then head west on Walk X route into **Castaño del Robledo**.

We start out from the square (**Bar Avenida**, Wp.1 0M) to walk back up the N433 main road (SSE) and take the second *camino* on our right, 'Camino de Galaroza a Castaño del Robledo' (Wp.2 4M). Our *camino* drops steeply down from the road (S) and the gradient eases for us to stroll along the cobbled trail to a *camino particular* and a waypost, where our route swings right.

The cobbles give way to a dirt surface as we come down to a ford and bridge (Wp.3 8M). Once across the **Río Múrgia** the cobbling returns for us to climb up past **Finca La Farruca** on our right, trees providing welcome shade as we pass another large house on our left just before the cobbling ends, where we step over a water channel (Wp.4 19M) onto a dirt trail.

The water-eroded dirt trail climbs through woodland to a waymarking post (Wp.5) and a decision. Just before the waypost a narrower trail sneaks (S) up through the broom and lavender to pass an old hut and a large barn on our right before coming through the trees onto the **Camino del Puerto** (Wp.6 27M), **Camino de Jabugo a Fuenteheridos** and **Camino de Pedregal**, all three waypostos together on a broad track.

Eight minutes into the route

The narrow trail is our preferred route, but we have found it blocked by cut branches. If in doubt about this access. then continue on the main trail until it meets the broad track further west and then turn east to stroll along to Wp.6, easily recognisable by the trio of wayposts.

Heading east, we stroll down to cross a watercourse that's piped under the track, after which it is steadily uphill on the comfortable surface between orchards of pollarded chestnuts enlivened by birdsong. We pass occasional wayposts and huts set amongst the trees, a potato plot providing something different on our way up to a cross roads of tracks (Wp.7 42M); here the **Camino de Jabugo a Fuenteheridos** is signed straight on by a waypost.

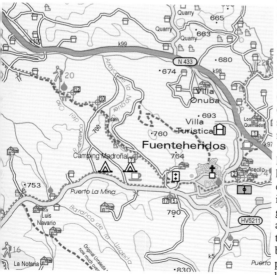

It's more of the same as we head east to a junction (Wp.8 46M), where a track goes right to **Castaño del Robledo** and links with Walk 16 just before the 'mustard' house (Wp.9) whose tiled terrace can make for a pleasant seat provided the house is not occupied.

Leaving the 'mustard' house behind we continue east along the track to an impressive but unnamed, gate entrance (Wp.10) after which the nature of the route changes. We begin to drop down past pines and a hut on the bulldozed track, followed

The mustard house at Wp.9

by a short climb onto a rise above a sharp valley across from an old *cortijo*. Following the track down into the valley, we come to a rushing watercourse (Wp.11 57M) crossed on a pair of logs, where a really rough track climbs the eastern valley to the old *cortijo*.

Here is where we need to have faith as the route is little walked, and paths quickly disappear amongst the vigorous plant growth on the valley floor. We head south alongside the stream (on our right) following a small path that crosses a tree-shaded meadow. We climb gently through bracken (Wp.12 60M) before stepping over a cut tree, our path reducing to a way at times as we head towards an old barn which we pass on the west (Wp.13 65M).

Our path becomes clearer beyond the hut, as we come amongst some of the oldest and most gnarled chestnut boles, the shady woodland now ancient and mysterious. We keep heading south to pass an old barn on our right (Wp.14) as we start climbing more steeply beside the stream, replaced by fencing as we climb through the trees to a fence ahead (Wp.15 75M). We swing left on a way, or making a way, alongside the fence as it climbs steeply up the eastern side of the valley to a shady tree, where we go right to walk up to the H7015 road by an old fence gate (Wp.16 82m) opposite the 'Recreación de Dañas y Infrastructuras Agrarías'.

On the quiet road we head east overlooking the forest and with views to the distant *sierras*, passing the **Jose Luís Navarrio** farm on our right, and **Los Molinos** house on our left, before climbing up through pines. Over the crest, we are back to easy strolling over a smaller rise and start to pass the **El Madroñal** camping area, after which there's a private track off to the right before we reach a junction of dirt roads on the north of the road (Wp.17 114M).

Here, we take the track which climbs to our front left, to come up a rise and swing left to come in front of the cemetery (Wp.18) with its ghoulish 'skull and crossbones' decoration. From the cemetery we follow the cobbled road down past the **Ermita de Señora Veronica** to the first houses. At the first street junction (Wp.19) we follow the 'Plaza el Coso' sign down to the right; yes, the directions even apply to walkers as well as drivers, and at the end of the street we go left at the T-junction we continue downhill on the cobbled street to emerge onto the **Plaza el Coso** opposite the famous **Fuente de los Doce Caños** (126M).

A strolling route through cork oak meadows, until the land abruptly changes as we approach **Cortelazor**, where the meadows are replaced by the cistus-covered shale slopes which mark the boundary between the rich farming of the *sierra* and the poorer grazing to the north.

Our route follows the **Camino Rural de Cortelazor** that serves the isolated farmsteads and *fincas* of the region, and consequently has numerous turnoffs to confuse the unwary. The *camino* has been recently upgraded, and technically you could drive along it, except for the centre section which is the least maintained and only passable by walkers, cyclists and the toughest of four wheel drive vehicles.

Access by Car
Park at the **Hotel Villa Turística** junction or car park, and walk along the north side of the main road to the start of the dirt track. If staying in **Fuenteheridos** either walk down the tarmac road to the **Villa Turística** junction, or follow Walk 4 to the N433, and then walk down the north side of the main road to the second dirt road off to the north.

Short Walk Option
At Wp.8, take the right hand track to run along the north side of the valley and run into our Fuenteheridos-Los Marines route at **Finca la Deseada** and then stay on the track to climb up to the N433.

Our start point is beside the N433 just past the km 97 marker at the start of a well-stabilised dirt track heading north-east (Wp.1 0M). Leaving the main road behind, we are immediately surrounded by delightful rural countryside of cork oak meadows, relatively flat for easy strolling compared to many of our routes. We pass a minor track off to our right before coming to **Finca el Palomar** entrance (Wp.2) and a second minor track on our right before cresting a small rise to views over the northern valleys and *sierras*.

The rule of navigation is to keep to the main track at all junctions (unless we say otherwise) as we pass **Los Quemados** and a minor track off to our right (Wp.3) by a marvellously decayed chestnut bole. A gentle downhill stroll between earth banks takes us past an old barn and a track off to our left (Wp.4), followed by a gate entrance and track into the pines on our left. We crest a small rise and run down between pines (left) and chestnuts (right) on a section of cobbled trail (Wp.5).

The cobbling gives out as we come down to cross a ford and then gently climb up through the woods, passing a track off to our left (Wp.6) Our track, now concreted, climbs before it levels off and reverts to dirt, and we pass a track off to our right (Wp.7). The route undulates along between old pollarded chestnuts to come to a Y-junction (Wp.8 23M) where it would be easy to take the uphill track on the right which would take us back to our Fuenteheridos-Los Marines route. We go left, the track rising and then running gradually downhill past a field full of the yellow spikes of wild annual lupin (Lupinus luteus) to a split in the track. The splits meet up again at a small crossroads (Wp.9) where 'Los Barreros' is signed straight ahead, and appears to be the main track. Here, we keep left (N) to pass a track on our left, just before a steep climb to a crest between stone walls.

We come down past a house entrance on a rocky section of the track, and go past **Finca El Pozito** to a T-junction (Wp.10 34M) where both left and right look equally major. If you were to go left, the track would take you along past **Finca El Moro** to meet the **Navahermosa** road a kilometre north of the N433, a walking/biking alternative country route.

Going right (E), we pass a house on our right as the track narrows and becomes hemmed in by trees and briars, and come down to a ford (Wp.11) before rising steadily up to a junction which faces an open meadow (Wp.12 41M). Here, the main track goes straight ahead to eventually run out onto the **Cortelazor** road just over a kilometre north of **Los Marines** - yet another option; (see Alternative Finish at the end of the walk description).

We go left (N) over a gentle crest and head down into a classic *sierra* valley of cork oak meadows studded with wild flowers - a marked contrast with what's ahead, as after coming down to cross a water course (Wp.13) we face a shale ridge matted with low cistus bushes.

... a classic *sierra* valley ...

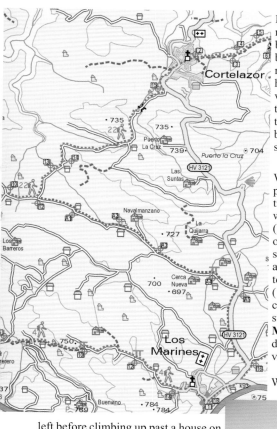

It's obvious that the ridge represents a boundary between two contrasting botanical and geological regions. So far, the route has been notable for its vibrant plant life, while on the ridge ahead, only the tenacious scrubby cistus bushes are tough enough to survive on the poor soil.

We set off up the track and past a farmhouse, the track's incline increasing; we stop at an elevated bend (Wp.14) for views back over the lush lands to the south. It's a gruelling ascent up through a bend , to arrive on top of the ridge (715 metres) for a comfortable high-level stroll overlooking the **Los Menores** valley before descending to cross the valley floor.

We pass a track off to our

.. views back over the lush lands to the south ...

left before climbing up past a house on our right. Up the ridge to its crest, and now the main climbs are behind us as we wind down the slopes to a brick bridge over a stream and then on to meet the **Los Marines** road (Wp.15 88M).

Once on the road, we could go uphill (!) and left for the back way into the town, but by now you would probably prefer walking <u>down</u> the road (N) to take the second cobbled street on the right (Wp.16 108M) which brings us into the church square with its options of **Bar Mano** and **Bar Plaza** for refreshments.

Alternative to finish in Los Marines

From the junction at Wp.12, we keep straight ahead on the main track, our route undulating along and passing a farm on our left (Wp.Alt1.) We stroll along to pass a second farm (Wp.Alt2) before climbing up from the meadows to the cistus-covered slopes. At a T-junction with a better stabilised track (Wp.Alt3) we go left (SE), to stride downhill back into farmland.

After passing a farm, we stroll between orchards to cross a stream with a nicely placed log seat (Wp.Alt4), for an optional break in these pleasant surroundings. From the seat we pass another farm on our right before coming onto the **Los Marines - Cortelazor** tarmac road (Wp.Alt5) where we turn right. Just over a kilometre of comfortable road walking brings us to the eastern outskirts of **Los Marines**.

This is one of our favourite trails in the Sierra de Aracena, demanding a string of adjectives including 'unspoiled', 'scenic' and 'floriferous', as we take what in local terms is a commuting route between the small town of **Cortelazor** and the tiny hamlet of **Corterrangel**. Wild flowers in abundance, an old cobbled trail mostly in good repair, beautiful landscapes and enough ascents and descents to feel you have justified some refreshments at the end; all we'd ask for is a little *tipico* bar in **Corterrangel**, and it would be perfect.

Access by Car
Cortelazor's streets are wider than most in the region, so it might be feasible to park in the town square; otherwise there's roadside parking on the southern outskirts.

Short Walk
To the **Ribeira Guijarra** valley and return. (2 walker 1 hour)

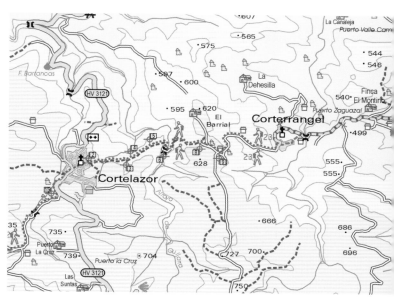

From the town square by the **Iglesia de Nuestra Señora de los Remedios** church (Wp.1 0M) we head (ENE) down an unnamed cobbled street (not the Calle Virgin de los Remedios) past traditional houses, some in course of renovation, which give way to huts. We pass a children's play area on our right (Wp.2 3M), and the street narrows to a cobbled trail to head down past huts and fields to cross a small valley.

Our route divides the slopes; olives below and cork oaks above the trail. We meander along in a gentle downhill amongst the trees, a small uphill (Wp.3)

... multitudes of wild flowers ...

from a green corner temporarily interrupting the general descent. Views open up over the northern *sierras* as we climb up to a rock 'gate' through an outcrop (Wp.4), and then resume our easy strolling until the trail cuts through a low ridge (Wp.5 17M) where we overlook the **Guijarra** valley. Our trail's surface which has been earth since the 'gate', is once again cobbled as we start dropping down into the valley past a multitude of wild flowers. We come down onto a dirt track to swing left onto a bridge above the tree-stuffed valley of the **Ribeira Guijarra** (Wp.6 24M).

This beautiful watercourse and valley setting demand attention, so no one would blame you for stopping here at the limit of our Short Walk option. While contemplating this picturesque scene, you might also consider the most substantial bridge and its short section of dirt road. The road peters out into trails at both ends, so why build such a significant looking bridge in what is the middle of nowhere, as far as roads are concerned?

From the bridge, we pass a gate to continue along the dirt track that peters out into a trail that starts climbing steadily up the eastern wall of the valley to a junction (Wp.7) where a rock-stepped path cuts off a loop of the trail. We stay on the main cobbled trail to climb steadily up through steep flower meadows, meeting the top of the short cut at a second hairpin bend.

If you're taking breaks on this steep section - and we are fairly sure that you will - then you can use the excuse of the splendid view back over the valley to **Cortelazor**. The path splits into dirt or cobbled, both coming back together for us to toil up, reaching sloping meadows teeming with wild flowers where the cobbling finally gives way to dirt.

Up across the meadows we come to a junction (Wp.8 38M) alongside a substantial signboard structure, once part of the **El Barrial** camping grounds that used to occupy this site. We continue on the dirt track going right (SE) to stroll steadily up to another junction (Wp.9) on a saddle beside a long closed bar-restaurant. Now we head downhill on the good track with the houses of **Corterrangle** visible below us through the oak tree meadows.

We simply follow the track down to pass through a substantial gate entrance and swing left to face the first houses of **Corterrangel** and in a few steps we are in the cute **Plaza de Corterrangel** (Wp.10 55M); at the top of the *plaza* is a cobbled trail with a 'Salida a Cortelazor' street sign but, oddly, this is not an alternative return route.

This little *aldea* was in danger of becoming abandoned until quite recently, but the growing interest in weekender homes has regenerated the hamlet, despite the closure of the camping ground above the settlement (Wps.8 & 9). Having come down as far as **Corterrangel**, it's worth taking a stroll out along the tarmac access road to its rural church, unusually set outside the hamlet amongst meadows .

Our return is unfortunately back up that dirt track, a trudging, toiling ascent; more like a penance than a pleasure until we reach the pass again (Wp.9) from where it's pure pleasure all the way back to the *plaza* in **Cortelazor**.

Plaza de Corterrangel

If we have to choose one single route that includes as much as possible of the attractiveness of the Sierra de Aracena, this is it. Ancient cobbled trails combine with the region's best *mirador* viewpoints, quiet country trails and hamlets plus the odd surprise to make a glorious day's hike. There is a little road walking, but only just over a kilometre, to complete our circuit based on **Almonaster la Real**.

This is the nearest we have to a traditional 'mountain' route but the one disappointing aspect is that you, and Uncle Tom Cobbley and all, can drive up the **Cerro de San Cristobal** on a narrow tarmac lane. If you wish to avoid arriving on the top hot and bothered to find yourself amongst family picnics, then walk this circuit on a weekday.

Short Walk Options

This route lends itself to so many shorter alternatives that we suggest just a few options:-

Take our outward route up to the *miradors* then return by the tarmac lane; this can be shortened even further by taking the 'open ground' short cut to the lane signed from the southern *mirador*.

Take our route until you come to the A470 above **Arroyo** and then walk down the road to **Almonaster**.

The **Porrejona** river valley could be walked as a separate route. Park at **Arroyo** and follow main route until you come back to the A470, then walk north up the road back to your start point.

Access by Car

Park on the entrance street to **Almonaster la Real**, alongside the A470, or in the parking area off the A470 above the town.

Unofficially, our start point is on the terrace of the **Hotel Casa García**, from where we walk down the A470 (E) to the edge of the town where we find a waymarked trail (Wp.1 0M) with a signboard 'Cerro de San Cristóbal 5.6km, 3 hours, medium/high difficulty'; this refers to the circular route shown on the board (our first Short Walk option). We set off up a cobbled donkey trail to the **Molinos Harineros**, an impressively big ruin of an old mill - go through the wall for better views of what was once the 'industrial' heart of this area.

Continuing up the immaculately preserved cobbled trail, we pass a public wash area (Wp.2) and two weekender cottages. We've been climbing steadily, but now our trail twists steeply upwards through ruined walls to arrive at a log

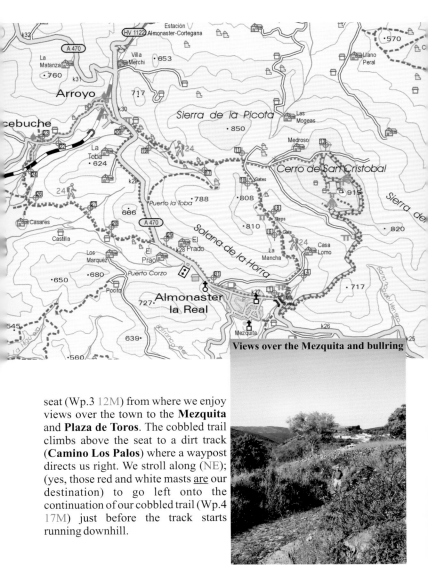

Views over the Mezquita and bullring

seat (Wp.3 12M) from where we enjoy views over the town to the **Mezquita** and **Plaza de Toros**. The cobbled trail climbs above the seat to a dirt track (**Camino Los Palos**) where a waypost directs us right. We stroll along (NE); (yes, those red and white masts <u>are</u> our destination) to go left onto the continuation of our cobbled trail (Wp.4 17M) just before the track starts running downhill.

Our cobbled trail climbs steeply until the gradient reduces to steady and the cobbles give way to dirt until a further cobbled ascent brings us up to another 'Cerro de San Cristóbal' signboard (Wp.5) with geological information (in Spanish). We've been ascending through a wild environment, but now our trail climbs up above olives and a potato plot, the property above our route displaying an old wooden sign for **La Mancha**. A gentle downhill takes us through the remains of an old gate and then it is a gentle ascent above the olive orchard, our trail lined by an avenue of cork oaks.

Stones litter our route as we come up to another old gate (Wp.6 30M) where the trail goes up to the left of the gate, climbing through trees and undergrowth with a stream down on our right, a set of wooden steps leading down to a stream-side dell (Wp.7). Orchids and wild garlic line the path as we come up to a thoughtfully sited wooden seat (Wp.8 35M) just before a muddy stream crossing with a wooden handrail.

At a waypost there is a confusion of trails; ours is, of course, steeply upwards on wooden steps which follow a stone wall to bring us alongside a gully, which we cross onto a dirt track (Wp.9). Here we go right (N), to a sign in a chestnut grove (in Spanish) advising us to go north/north-west through the grove. We follow the trail (N) to a waypost where the trail swings to north-west, bringing us up to another waypost beside a pair of old wooden gates (Wp.10). Through the gates, our trail joins a track for us to stroll down (a relief after all that climbing) to a track junction (Wp.11 55M).

At the junction a trail, marked with faded *PR* waymark goes left (W) for our circular return, **Almonaster la Real** is signed back down the trail we have climbed, and a waypost directs us right. Going right, we walk up the orange-ochre track, gradually ascending through oaks to come into the open by a gated track crossroads (Wp.12) with the summit ahead of us.

As we climb the track, the trees are replaced by high shrubbery and views open up over **Cortegana** where the growth allows. This final ascent to the summit ought to be a pleasant stroll, but the track is just steep enough to require rest stops, whereupon flies emerge from the dense shrubbery to feed on the static walker; break off a small branch early in this ascent so you can combat the flies when you stop, or pace yourself not to stop on this section. A final steep section of track brings us trudging up to the tarmac lane by a waypost (Wp.13 72M); the track continues eastwards, dropping down towards **Los Romeros**.

Heading south on the tarmac, we have a gentle stroll up to a junction (Wp.14 76M) for a choice of *mirador* viewpoints. Continuing straight ahead (S), the tarmac gives out by the aerials and their huts for us to stroll over to the southern *mirador* (Wp.15 915 metres) where an alternative descent for those who want to short cut down to the tarmac lane is marked by a waypost.

View from the southern *mirador*

Views from the *mirador* are amongst the best in the *sierras*, so take your time. A signboard explaining what you can see has unfortunately been defaced, but gives a general idea of the towns and ridges. If only this spot was maintained, and the seats placed for the views along with a recreation area perhaps, this could be one of the most popular spots in the region. There's an impression that the authorities are giving lip-service to tourism, but not really embracing this alien concept. This view, though not the physical view, is repeated at the northern *mirador* (Wp.16) where a hut for the 'Junta de Andalucia' seems both redundant and sited to clash with the natural environment.

Return routes

We have a choice of routes for our return to **Almonaster la Real**; we can **(a)** follow the waypost from the southern *mirador* to the tarmac lane (adventurous, and the quickest route), **(b)** stroll down the tarmac lane (comfortable and easy), **(c)** return by our outward route revisiting the beautiful valley and ruins, or **(d)** take our long adventurous circuit, taking in **Arroyo** and **Acebuche** which adds yet another perspective to the route.

The long adventurous return route

We return to the junction at Wp.11 (17M), an easy strolling descent in contrast to our slogging ascent up the track. Here we take the old **Cortegana** trail (W) marked with old *PR* waymarking. It's a narrow trail with vigorous plant growth pushing in on this little-walked route - secateurs are definitely recommended to help keep this way open. It's a steady descent, becoming steeper on cobbled sections, with careful footwork required on the stone-littered surface.

We experience the endemic plant life in extreme close-up until a meadow opens up beside our trail (Wp.17 30M) and we thankfully exchange the pushing through scratchy plants for a woodland path. Descending through the trees and scrub, we pass beneath a hut and then above a small ruin before the path widens out (Wp.18) beside a stone wall, the gradient easing from the knee-jarring descent we've had so far.

The trail is still rock-littered as we cross a small stream before continuing down the rock-stepped route, cobbled on the steeper sections, to be joined by a small canal (Wp.19 46M) at a junction where a path follows the canal back into the valley on our left. Passing beneath a corral and hut, we come into the open to head towards a white house where the house driveway leads us onto the A470 road (Wp.20 52M) by a bus shelter. If you want to shortcut back to **Almonaster la Real** from this point, turn left and follow the road to join our main route in approximately 25 minutes, 1.5 kilometres, of steady walking.

After that long 'picky' descent the situation rapidly improves as we cross the 'main' road (0M) to stroll down the minor road and pass above **Arroyo**'s tiny square. We pass houses strung along the road before coming down to shady seating by the public wash area (Wp.21), a pleasant setting if you wish to take a break. Leaving **Arroyo** behind, we stroll down the little-used road to the first house of **Acebuche** (Wp.22) by the village sign. Houses begin to line the road, and just before they end we take a cobbled street (Wp.23 17M) to our left (S) opposite a donkey trail (the *GR* route to **Cortegana**).

This marble-cobbled street illustrates the regeneration now taking place in the region. As we stroll south, it's clear that new houses fill in significant numbers of plots not occupied by traditional houses, many of which have been upgraded and modernised. A neat primary school complements the houses, and all that is missing is a friendly *tipico* bar. Checking our directions for **Almonaster la Real** with a local, he gave us the advice to "keep left and keep keeping left", very useful advice as it turned out.

The first railway crossing sign

At the end of the houses the street runs out into a trail, for us to drop down past huts to an excessively large 'Tren' railway crossing sign, apparently marooned amongst the trees - surely a joke; but not so, as the trail does indeed bring us down to overlook the railway line. At a junction we 'keep left' to drop down and cross the railway line (Wp.24 24M), and continue on the narrow trail through briars and a muddy section before coming into a meadow and another 'Tren' sign; looking back, we have views of the water tunnel under the railway. Past the sign, our route is confirmed by a *GR* waymark just before we drop down to meet the river and a stone-laid trail. We have to walk along the river bed (difficult to keep dry feet) to reach the boulder-laid donkey trail (Wp.25) and climb steeply up to a junction with old waymarking on the stone wall (Wp.26 41M).

Interesting walking trails run ahead and front right, approximately south, but remembering the local advice, we go left to climb up to pass between gated pastures heading east towards tree-covered hills before swinging right (SE) above an olive grove.

We come down to a stream crossing (Wp.27 54M), then climb through a woodland/bush landscape, keeping to the main trail whenever minor paths and traces run off into the trees. Passing beside a house set in the woods (Wp.28 64M), we go past its sheep's bell entrance gate, our trail becoming more defined as we climb up alongside a lichen covered wall. The route levels out at a water runoff before resuming its ascent. Swinging right above a hut, we cross a stream into an area which shows more signs of cultivation, passing a cave door below a cork oak just before the A470 crash barriers come into sight above us. A final climb brings us up onto the 'main' road (Wp.29 77M).

Our finish is an easy stroll up past the farmsteads of **El Prao** (on the right) and **El Prado** (on the left) to the showy *cementerio* (Wp.30) on the crest of the road, from where it's gently downhill past **Ermita de la Señora de la Humildad** set on the junction with the first street into the town (Wp.31). Our choice is to keep to strolling down the 'main' road for a choice of **Bar/Rest El Rincón de Curra** (Wp.32 90M) or the more distant terrace of **Hotel Casa García** for refreshments.

By far the most delightful exit from **Cortegana** but unfortunately the old route has been cut by the new N433 main road; this aside we have a beautiful tour along the **Fuente de los Berros** valley. The original route approaching **La Posada** has been lost, requiring us to follow a newer and more difficult path (secateurs recommended on this section) before arriving at the hotel.

Combine the route with Walk 26 La Pousada-Cortegana for a long circular, or with Walk 27 Los Molinos-Cortegana for a shorter circular.

2/3 · 1½ H · 6 km · 50m / 270m · 4

Access by car

Park off the N433 main road taking the first left into the town if arriving from the east and park near the road up to the *castillo* in **Cortegana** or around the small square - actually a triangle. **Bar la Glorieta** faces the triangle, but its few sticks of furniture and distressed interior decoration are reminiscent of the remnants in a spaghetti western saloon after the big fight.

Starting from the square/triangle (Wp.1 0M) we walk steadily up the road (SW) past shops and houses until reaching the **Panificadora Cortegana** (Wp.2) where we go left and uphill along a street with overhanging balconies, and then turn right to come down to the church; you could reach this point a bit quicker by going straight on at the **Panificadora**. Past the church, we leave the cobbled street to go down pedestrian steps (Wp.3) which widen to a street heading downhill (SSE). We pass a *fuente* and

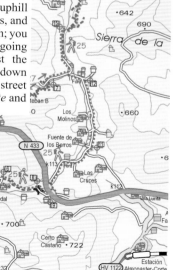

cobbled road on our right before coming to a T-junction at the end of **Peñas** (Wp.4). Going right, the street (signed as a cul-de-sac) reduces to a cobbled track as we leave the town behind.

We have fine views of the castle as we descend between banks of briars, passing gated entrances before coming to a surreal collection of boulders in a plot on our left (Wp.5) along with a mill wheel set in the wall. Horses and sheep graze the flower-filled meadows on our right, as we come to the end of the track at **El Guindal**'s entrance (Wp.6).

Ahead, a cobbled trail drops towards the river for a careful descent on the slippery surface, flora pushing in on our route as the sounds of churning water come up to greet us. The cobbles are overgrown with clover and grass as we lose height and pass a telegraph post (Wp.7) with *GR* markings. We come to the stream opposite a cottage and outbuildings across the water. Our trail, now dirt, pushes through grasses on the left bank of the *arroyo* to an old brick bridge (Wp.8 28M) which once carried the main road.

The earth bank supporting the N433 has cut the old 'classic' route, so we divert up the old road to the N433 (Wp.9) and cross over onto a pair of dirt tracks and a tarmac lane. Taking the tarmac we drop down into the valley, the tarmac changing to dirt track as we contour along through this semi-cultivated landscape in an easy stroll, to swing right past buildings to a ford (Wp.10).

The stream crossing at 66 minutes

We climb up, passing **Las Cruces** on our right, and then we are contouring along past the entrance to **Fuente de los Berros** (Wp.11) and after a short climb, the entrances to **Esteban Benitez** and **Los Molinos**. Our well stabilised track runs along to a junction with a concrete track coming in from the right (Wp.12 53M) as we drop down to the left and pass the houses of the **Los Molinos** artists' colony, crossing the *arroyo* at a ford. Climbing up the trail, we ford a second fast running affluent (Wp.13) to meet the route of Walk 27, and a dirt track off to our right.

Taking the track (N) we pass a house before coming to a luxurious pig pen at the edge of woods (Wp.14) where the track ends and we continue into the woods on a narrow trail. Our route has been getting more 'woody' for a little while, and now we're in a true woodland-nymph setting as the narrow trail winds amongst tall poplars (poor GPS reception) taking us along the left bank of the fast flowing stream. A slightly vertiginous section of the path takes us above a barrage protecting a water pipe from the stream's flow. We pass an electricity hut before coming to the remains of a mill (Wp.15 66M) where a 'crossed' *GR* sign warns us not to continue ahead.

Crossing to the right bank - difficult without getting wet, so probably best to accept the inevitable and simply wade across, we come to the yellow and white *GR* markings confirming our route's continuation. Our trail climbs up to overlook the stream, passing a path off to the right before coming to a junction (Wp.16) by a gated meadow where a path goes down towards the stream. Going through the 'wire' gate, yes this is the official route, confirmed to us by the swineherd, we stroll across the meadow to a second 'wire' gate; again there is a path heading down towards the stream as we keep straight ahead to pass below a barn set amongst the cork oaks.

The easy meadow strolling takes us past a *GR* marked stone wall (Wp.17) as our narrow trail meanders amongst the trees to come to an old mill on the opposite bank, the substantial stone structure now almost devoured by trees and briars (Wp.18 80M). Passing a *GR* marker, and a second mill ruin on the left bank, we come back to the stream by a barrage, and the most difficult section of the route.

The original stream crossing was swept away long ago and so a new path has been cut, first pushing through bracken and then into dense undergrowth where secateurs are a distinct advantage in opening up the tunnel. A fallen tree has to be scrambled under before we come to a section of wire fence where a tricky drop releases us from the tangle beside a side stream and a *GR* sign. Climbing up from the side stream we are back on a boot-wide path following a stone wall on our right, and skirting a fallen tree as we wade through bracken to come back to the stream by a large tree with a *GR* marker directing us to cross to the left bank.

Tree felling has confused the left bank's trail, so head up away from the water to a 'wire' gate giving access onto a dirt track (Wp.19 95M), the route of Walk 26. Turning right, the chalet-style rooms of **La Posada** come into view below us, but before we reach this haven our track swings left above a valley to cross a ford (Wp.20), before swinging back to drop down to the hotel entrance (Wp.21 99M). The bar/restaurant at **La Posada** is open during normal walking hours, and makes for a pleasant break from fighting with the undergrowth.

26 LA POSADA - CORTEGANA
(The Big Hill)

If you are fortunate enough to be staying at **La Posada** then (after a hearty breakfast) this is the route for you to walk into the hill fort town of **Cortegana**; though if you do set out straight after breakfast, expect to take a bit longer than our one hour. It's all uphill, but through beautiful countryside on tracks and trails until we reach the scruffy suburb of **Cortegana**.

Link with routes 25, and/or 27 to make a day's circular exploration.

From the hotel entrance, we start out from the deceptive 'PRA3 Cortegana 2km' sign (Wp.1 0M) - the track does go to **Cortegana** but it's not two kilometres - to walk up the dirt track as it swings across a ford (Wp.2) before we curve up above the hotel's chalets to pass the wire gate of Walk 25 (Wp.3). It is gently uphill past cork oak studded meadows, our route paralleling Walk 25 but in much easier circumstances on the gentle dirt track.

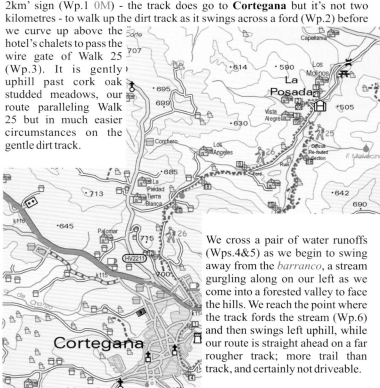

We cross a pair of water runoffs (Wps.4&5) as we begin to swing away from the *barranco*, a stream gurgling along on our left as we come into a forested valley to face the hills. We reach the point where the track fords the stream (Wp.6) and then swings left uphill, while our route is straight ahead on a far rougher track; more trail than track, and certainly not driveable.

Much of the cobbling on our trail has been swept away by water erosion, as we climb steadily (W) between sloping meadows and forest, with a solar powered house sitting atop a knoll away on our right. It's onwards and upwards on the eroded trail to pass a crumbling hut (Wp.7 28M) before we overlook two houses set in the valley.

Meeting the access track to the houses (Wp.8), we come onto a better stabilised track - not that there is much relaxing as it is still relentlessly uphill, except when we take breaks to marvel at the bucolic tranquility of the valley. A bubbling stream runs along the side of our track, bands of rock creating numerous small waterfalls, as we come amongst the trees to pass a spring (Wp.9).

We are still climbing until we reach the pass with gate entrances left and right (Wp.10 41M) where we leave the track to take a cobbled trail on our front left marked by an old *PR* yellow and white paint mark. Our boulder-cobbled trail, dating from Roman times, twists steeply up through the trees and though steep, it's easier than trudging up the dirt track. Coming to a gate entrance, and an adventurous path up to our left, we are now on a driving width track (Wp.11 48M) which continues uphill for us to walk beneath a stone and brick built barn set above a corner of the track.

The Roman boulder-cobbled trail

At last we come over a crest, the first houses of **Cortegana** coming into view ahead, to the unfortunate sight of a large rubbish tip. We pass a trail off to our right (Wp.12), running up to an antennaed peak if you've the desire and energy to explore it. At a junction (Wp.13) we come onto a wider track serving scruffy buildings in the eastern valley, while we walk up past the rubbish to come up to the first houses at the start of a concrete street (Wp14), the view of the castle ahead a welcome contrast to the rubbish heap behind us on this section.

We stroll down the wide street, lined by tenements and small houses, seeking a suitable *tipico* for some refreshments; **Bar/Restaurant Los Paroles** (Wp.15) looks the best but is passed too early. There are a couple more distressed *tipicos* towards the end of the street but not sufficiently attractive to tempt us in, just after which we pass a parking area on our right, and so we reach the end of our route at the main road (Wp.16 68M) to settle for water from our back packs.

A delightful woodland route, once you have got past the unpromising start, but it is steep; tough on the knees in descent and tough on everything in ascent. You can link this route with our Classic route as a more direct way to **La Posada**, or as a circular excursion in the upper valley.

*25 minutes down, 40 minutes up

Access by Car

Park on the road or at the parking area just to the north of the main road, first right at **Cortegana** if arriving from the east.

Our starting point is on the northern side of the main road through **Cortegana** where just by the crash barrier is a *PR* symbol (Wp.1/46 0M) where we take a path which parallels the road, endemic flora battling the litter as we curve down to pass a concrete hut with a *PR* symbol and come onto a dirt track (Wp.2/49 4M).

Keeping left, our track curves over a crest and leaves that unpromising start behind as we start dropping down into a valley between slopes of cork oaks and olives. We come down past gate entrances and a *PR* symbol (Wp.3/50) where a path goes left as we keep straight ahead, the track narrowing to trail width as it heads downhill. Keeping to the main trail, we come down past another *PR* symbol to rather grand entrance gates (Wp.4/53 10M); so perhaps it is driveable to here, but certainly no further than the **Esteban B** gates (Wp.5/54).

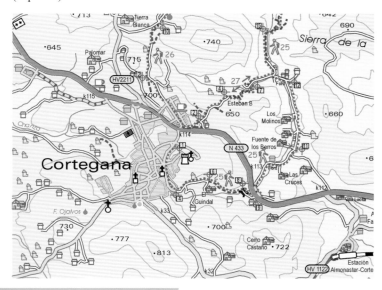

Now it is a much eroded cobbled trail down through the lush vegetation and hairpin bend, to walk above a stream that we can hear but not see until we swing left (Wp.6/56) to cross the water on stepping stones. A *PR* symbol confirms our route as the trail undulates along between an earth bank and tall lichen-covered trees to join a dirt track (Wp.7/57). Keeping downhill, the sounds of the river greet us as we pass cultivated plots before coming down to the junction (Wp.8/59 25M) with our Classic route to **La Posada**.

down through lush vegetation ...

For **La Posada** take the trail to the left (N), while for a circular back to **Cortegana** continue on the track over the river and follow our classic route back to the town.

GPS Waypoints for the 27 walking routes included in Sierra de Aracena - a Walk! Guidebook are quoted in Latitude/Longitude for the WGS84 Datum; the default datum for GPS receivers. Before loading waypoints into your GPS unit please read 'Using GPS in the Sierra de Aracena' on page 35. To input the waypoints into your GPS set the 'location format' to 'hddd° .mm.mmm´ and check that your datum is set to WGS84. While we quote waypoints to four places of decimals, as recorded during our research, you might only be able to input to three places of decimals, depending upon your GPS unit. In this case round the third decimal place to the nearest number; e.g. .0178 would be rounded to .018, while .9224 would be rounded to .922.

Full GPS Track and Waypoint files for these 27 walking routes, in Oziexplorer format files, are available on our PNFs (Personal Navigator Files) CD available for £7.99 from Discovery Walking Guides Ltd. See our websites for more information:-
www.walking.demon.co.uk and www.dwgwalking.co.uk

1. ARACENA - CORTECONCEPCIÓN NORTH

Wp	N	W
1	37 53.6514	6 33.6576
2	37 53.7702	6 33.5106
3	37 53.9484	6 33.2622
4	37 54.0150	6 33.0000
5	37 54.1272	6 32.8074
6	37 54.1440	6 32.3826
7	37 54.2016	6 32.1426
8	37 54.2082	6 31.8882
9	37 54.2370	6 31.8396
10	37 54.2388	6 31.8162
11	37 54.1596	6 31.4760
12	37 53.9682	6 31.1076
13	37 53.8836	6 30.9366
14	37 53.8056	6 30.8094
15	37 53.8914	6 30.6150

2. CORTECONCEPCIÓN - ARACENA

Wp	N	W
1	37 53.8914	6 30.6150
2	37 53.8356	6 30.6720
3	37 53.8056	6 30.8094
4	37 53.6874	6 31.2120
5	37 53.5842	6 31.3938
6	37 53.5536	6 31.5702
7	37 53.6724	6 31.8510
8	37 53.6982	6 32.0058
9	37 53.6832	6 32.2044
10	37 53.6388	6 32.5992
11	37 53.6166	6 32.8938
12	37 53.5956	6 32.9442
13	37 53.5434	6 33.1692
14	37 53.5338	6 33.4386
15	37 53.6514	6 33.6576

3. ARACENA - LOS MARINES

Wp	N	W
1	37 53.6688	6 33.6678
2	37 53.7864	6 33.7230
3	37 53.8776	6 34.0704
4	37 53.9508	6 34.1436
5	37 54.1974	6 34.5522
6	37 54.2550	6 34.7592
7	37 54.1650	6 35.0130
8	37 54.1302	6 35.1468
9	37 54.1266	6 35.2716
10	37 54.1782	6 35.4978
11	37 54.1962	6 35.6472
12	37 54.2250	6 35.7732
13	37 54.2376	6 36.0570
14	37 54.2994	6 36.2334
15	37 54.4512	6 36.5400
16	37 54.3288	6 37.0044
17	37 54.2244	6 37.0992
18	37 54.1218	6 37.3014

4. FUENTEHERIDOS - LOS MARINES

Wp	N	W
1	37 54.2172	6 39.6294
2	37 54.2232	6 39.4800
3	37 54.3144	6 39.1554
4	37 54.4350	6 38.8914
5	37 54.4398	6 38.7672
6	37 54.4416	6 38.6742
7	37 54.4458	6 38.5782
8	37 54.4440	6 38.5110
9	37 54.4182	6 38.3796
10	37 54.4074	6 38.2104
11	37 54.4140	6 37.9674
12	37 54.3600	6 37.8372
13	37 54.2844	6 37.7100
14	37 54.1806	6 37.5648
15	37 54.1806	6 37.4244

5. LOS MARINES - LINARES DE LA SIERRA

Wp	N	W
1	37 54.1218	6 37.3014
2	37 53.8794	6 37.6038
3	37 53.8428	6 37.6026
4	37 53.7516	6 37.6206
5	37 53.6016	6 37.5396
6	37 53.5698	6 37.4970
7	37 53.5512	6 37.4238
8	37 53.5392	6 37.2240
9	37 53.3844	6 37.1022
10	37 53.2470	6 36.9660
11	37 53.1474	6 36.9066
12	37 53.0946	6 36.8994
13	37 53.0370	6 36.8358
14	37 52.9968	6 36.9030
15	37 52.8762	6 37.0788
16	37 52.8114	6 37.1694
17	37 52.8084	6 37.2672

6. LINARES DE LA SIERRA - ARACENA (Steep Route)

Wp	N	W
1	37 52.8084	6 37.2672
2	37 52.8336	6 37.2096
3	37 52.8114	6 37.1694
4	37 53.0046	6 36.8796
5	37 53.0370	6 36.8358
6	37 53.0250	6 36.7986
7	37 53.0658	6 36.7200
8	37 52.9506	6 36.0648
9	37 52.9710	6 36.0258
10	37 53.0574	6 35.8260
11	37 53.0490	6 35.6004
12	37 53.0820	6 35.3496
13	37 53.0976	6 35.0220
14	37 53.1882	6 34.7538
15	37 53.2626	6 34.4688
16	37 53.3694	6 34.3026
17	37 53.4450	6 34.0968

7. LINARES DE LA SIERRA - ARACENA (Southern Route)

Wp	N	W
1	37 52.8276	6 37.3326
2	37 52.6470	6 37.1568
3	37 52.5576	6 37.0566
4	37 52.4796	6 36.8214
5	37 52.4832	6 36.4332
6	37 52.3542	6 36.1500
7	37 52.3170	6 36.0942
8	37 52.2138	6 35.8536
9	37 52.2426	6 35.6856
10	37 52.3116	6 35.5428
11	37 52.3740	6 35.4678
12	37 52.5408	6 35.3370
13	37 52.5888	6 35.2662
14	37 52.6866	6 35.0994
15	37 52.8072	6 34.9464
16	37 52.9254	6 34.8468
17	37 53.1162	6 34.4400
18	37 53.1960	6 34.3182
19	37 53.2950	6 34.4130

8. LINARES DE LA SIERRA - RIVER ROUTE

Wp	N	W
1	37 52.8264	6 37.3350
2	37 52.7540	6 37.2672
3	37 52.7082	6 37.2186
4	37 52.6452	6 37.1574
5	37 52.6206	6 37.1940
6	37 52.3368	6 37.2900
7	37 52.2918	6 37.2918
8	37 52.2222	6 37.2444
9	37 51.9948	6 37.3392
10	37 51.7284	6 37.1520

9. ALÁJAR - LINARES DE LA SIERRA via LOS MADROÑEROS

Wp	N	W
1	37 52.5246	6 39.6198
2	37 52.4916	6 39.7062
3	37 52.4742	6 39.7674
4	37 52.4712	6 39.8250
5	37 52.4322	6 39.8700
6	37 52.3464	6 39.7566
7	37 52.3182	6 39.6372
8	37 52.3056	6 39.5646
9	37 52.2858	6 39.5106
10	37 52.2288	6 39.4008
11	37 52.1736	6 39.4068
12	37 52.0386	6 39.2064
13	37 51.9678	6 38.9784
14	37 51.9660	6 38.9166
15	37 51.9474	6 38.8752
16	37 51.9720	6 38.8692
17	37 52.0404	6 38.5632
18	37 52.1274	6 38.4012
19	37 52.1904	6 38.2602
20	37 52.3068	6 38.1702
21	37 52.4202	6 38.0088
22	37 52.4364	6 37.8900
23	37 52.5750	6 37.4304
24	37 52.6596	6 37.3860
25	37 52.7442	6 37.3440
26	37 52.7544	6 37.3656
27	37 52.7958	6 37.4148

10. LINARES DE LA SIERRA - ALÁJAR (Steep Route)

Wp	N	W
1	37 52.7958	6 37.4148
2	37 52.7526	6 37.9002
3	37 52.8168	6 38.2512
4	37 52.8660	6 38.5602
5	37 52.8498	6 38.7462
6	37 52.8408	6 38.7714
7	37 52.8156	6 38.8482
8	37 52.8000	6 38.9478
9	37 52.7274	6 39.2052
10	37 52.6836	6 39.3198
11	37 52.5246	6 39.6198

11. ALÁJAR - CASTAÑO DEL ROBLEDO

Wp	N	W
1	37 52.4442	6 40.1766
2	37 52.4556	6 40.3914
3	37 52.5462	6 40.4964
4	37 52.5198	6 40.5954
5	37 52.5582	6 40.7232
6	37 52.5966	6 40.8702
7	37 52.6722	6 40.9356
8	37 52.7586	6 41.0268
9	37 52.8336	6 41.1246
10	37 52.8804	6 41.1336
11	37 53.1930	6 41.5662
12	37 53.2908	6 41.6814
13	37 53.3496	6 41.7180
14	37 53.5050	6 41.8362
15	37 53.6346	6 41.8722
16	37 53.7378	6 42.1824
17	37 53.7126	6 42.2256

12. CASTAÑO DEL ROBLEDO - SANTA ANA LA REAL

Wp	N	W
1	37 53.7126	6 42.2256
2	37 53.6574	6 42.3342
3	37 53.5836	6 42.3270
4	37 53.4240	6 42.3666
5	37 53.0088	6 42.2736
6	37 52.9434	6 42.2748
7	37 52.7664	6 42.3288
8	37 52.4550	6 42.5490
9	37 52.4448	6 42.5766
10	37 52.4034	6 42.6744
11	37 52.3464	6 42.7278
12	37 52.2846	6 42.6138
13	37 52.1844	6 42.5172
14	37 51.9228	6 42.9684
15	37 51.8676	6 43.1580
16	37 51.8928	6 43.3290
17	37 51.8460	6 43.4664
E1	37 52.3355	6 42.9240
E2	37 52.1506	6 42.9636
E3	37 52.0096	6 42.8291

13. SANTA ANA LA REAL - ALÁJAR

Wp	N	W
1	37 51.8460	6 43.4664
2	37 51.8928	6 43.3290
3	37 51.8576	6 43.1780
4	37 51.8112	6 42.8304
5	37 51.7860	6 42.6828
6	37 51.7446	6 42.3324
7	37 51.7434	6 42.0690
8	37 51.7086	6 41.8914
9	37 51.7440	6 41.7522
10	37 51.8280	6 41.5800
11	37 51.8244	6 41.4714
12	37 51.9894	6 41.0418
13	37 51.8946	6 40.8798
14	37 51.9180	6 40.8204
15	37 51.9234	6 40.7826
16	37 52.1688	6 40.6494
17	37 52.2300	6 40.5132
18	37 52.2126	6 40.4772
19	37 52.2462	6 40.3932
20	37 52.3884	6 40.0512

15. PEÑA DE ARIAS MONTANO

Wp	N	W
1	37 52.6566	6 40.0788
2	37 52.6506	6 40.1574
3	37 52.6866	6 40.2948
4	37 52.7934	6 40.2750
5	37 52.8480	6 40.2240
6	37 52.8180	6 40.1478

17. GALAROZA - JABUGO - RIBEIRA DE JABUGO - GALAROZA

Wp	N	W
1	37 55.5138	6 42.9438
2	37 55.5000	6 42.9924
3	37 55.5036	6 43.0500
4	37 55.4304	6 43.2822
5	37 55.2336	6 43.6638
6	37 54.8862	6 43.6224
7	37 54.7878	6 43.4982
8	37 54.5622	6 43.3890
9	37 54.5640	6 43.3158
10	37 54.4446	6 43.1700
11	37 54.6168	6 43.0704
12	37 54.8058	6 43.1094
13	37 55.1772	6 43.0764
14	37 55.2534	6 42.9468
15	37 55.3704	6 42.8052
16	37 55.4442	6 42.7170
17	37 55.4820	6 42.7158

14. LOS MADROÑEROS CIRCULAR

Wp	N	W
1	37 52.4406	6 40.1256
2	37 52.4664	6 39.9420
3	37 52.4484	6 39.9360
4	37 52.4346	6 39.8724
5	37 52.3494	6 39.7608
6	37 52.3086	6 39.5622
7	37 51.9684	6 38.9760
8	37 51.9546	6 38.9094
9	37 51.9078	6 38.9604
10	37 51.8604	6 39.1566
11	37 51.7950	6 39.1818
12	37 51.7542	6 39.1962
13	37 51.6462	6 39.3522
14	37 51.6912	6 39.3720
15	37 51.8376	6 39.6120
16	37 51.8862	6 39.8166
17	37 51.8886	6 40.0314
18	37 52.0182	6 40.0434
19	37 52.1688	6 40.0332
20	37 52.3308	6 39.9834
21	37 52.4328	6 39.9336
Alt1	37 52.4874	6 39.7062
Alt2	37 52.4646	6 39.6900
Alt3	37 52.4364	6 39.7032
Alt4	37 52.3494	6 39.6408
Alt5	37 52.3230	6 39.6294
S1	37 51.9534	6 39.4164
S2	37 51.9660	6 39.1932

16. LA URRALEDA - CASTAÑO DEL ROBLEDO CIRCUIT

Wp	N	W
1	37 53.4006	6 39.7590
2	37 53.3784	6 39.8070
3	37 53.5476	6 40.3626
4	37 53.5824	6 40.4388
5	37 53.3088	6 41.0466
6	37 53.3886	6 41.1096
7	37 53.6172	6 41.1396
8	37 53.8710	6 41.5080
9	37 53.8920	6 41.8374
10	37 53.8962	6 41.9616
11	37 53.7678	6 42.1368
12	37 53.7336	6 42.1914
13	37 53.7114	6 42.2238
14	37 53.6436	6 41.8848
15	37 53.6286	6 41.8428
16	37 53.4588	6 41.7006
17	37 53.3898	6 41.7024
18	37 53.3370	6 41.6760
19	37 53.1942	6 41.5662
20	37 53.1798	6 41.4564
21	37 53.1480	6 41.4132
22	37 53.0196	6 41.0196
23	37 53.1360	6 41.0334

18. RIBEIRA DE JABUGO

Wp	N	W
1	37 55.4178	6 42.3798
2	37 55.4904	6 42.7140
3	37 55.4082	6 42.8688
4	37 55.3668	6 42.8970
5	37 55.2666	6 42.9474
6	37 55.1106	6 43.1496
7	37 54.8112	6 43.1040
8	37 54.6306	6 43.0704
9	37 54.4512	6 43.1430
10	37 54.4044	6 43.1628
11	37 54.2844	6 43.1220
12	37 54.1746	6 43.0596
13	37 54.0336	6 43.0152
14	37 53.9190	6 42.7206
15	37 53.7642	6 42.5298
16	37 53.7720	6 42.4284
17	37 53.7390	6 42.3264
18	37 53.7396	6 42.2748
19	37 53.7066	6 42.2322

19.
CASTAÑO DEL ROBLEDO - GALAROZA

Wp	N	W
1	37 53.7066	6 42.2322
2	37 53.7942	6 42.2412
3	37 53.8614	6 42.2088
4	37 53.8500	6 42.3432
5	37 54.0462	6 42.6174
6	37 54.3264	6 42.5724
7	37 54.4650	6 42.5838
8	37 54.7050	6 42.5286
9	37 54.7350	6 42.3366
10	37 54.9060	6 42.3516
11	37 55.1766	6 42.3504
12	37 55.2948	6 42.3354
13	37 55.4197	6 42.3807

20.
CAMINO DE GALAROZA

Wp	N	W
1	37 54.2098	6 39.6503
2	37 54.1806	6 39.7584
3	37 54.2334	6 39.8556
4	37 54.2268	6 39.9456
5	37 54.1782	6 40.0200
6	37 54.2850	6 40.0482
7	37 54.4038	6 40.2630
8	37 54.5022	6 40.4310
9	37 54.5772	6 40.4622
10	37 54.6324	6 40.5240
11	37 54.6630	6 40.6896
12	37 54.7314	6 40.7898
13	37 54.8076	6 40.8906
14	37 54.8508	6 41.0418
15	37 54.8910	6 41.1774
16	37 54.9708	6 41.2794
17	37 54.9762	6 41.3136
18	37 55.0296	6 41.4198
19	37 55.1268	6 41.6334
20	37 55.1430	6 41.6478
21	37 55.2600	6 41.8770
22	37 55.2936	6 42.3348
23	37 55.4316	6 42.3702

21.
CAMINO DE FUENTEHERIDOS

Wp	N	W
1	37 55.4316	6 42.3702
2	37 55.2936	6 42.3348
3	37 55.1760	6 42.3456
4	37 54.9696	6 42.2958
5	37 54.9054	6 42.3498
6	37 54.7392	6 42.3426
7	37 54.5482	6 41.9654
8	37 54.5652	6 41.7642
9	37 54.5748	6 41.7390
10	37 54.5640	6 41.6454
11	37 54.4020	6 41.4564
12	37 54.3156	6 41.4876
13	37 54.2130	6 41.5452
14	37 54.1206	6 41.5728
15	37 53.9742	6 41.5656
16	37 53.8746	6 41.5020
17	37 54.1782	6 40.0200
18	37 54.2268	6 39.9456
19	37 54.2334	6 39.8556

22.
FUENTEHERIDOS - CORTELAZOR

Wp	N	W
1	37 54.4470	6 39.3654
2	37 54.5700	6 39.3150
3	37 54.6450	6 39.3900
4	37 54.7836	6 39.4466
5	37 54.8466	6 39.3546
6	37 54.8694	6 39.2394
7	37 54.8976	6 39.1218
8	37 54.9666	6 38.9526
9	37 55.1376	6 38.9394
10	37 55.3260	6 38.7948
11	37 55.3008	6 38.7066
12	37 55.3110	6 38.5494
13	37 55.4826	6 38.4312
14	37 55.5354	6 38.3370
15	37 55.9996	6 37.6454
16	37 56.1073	6 37.5337
Alt1	37 55.2468	6 38.3100
Alt2	37 55.1460	6 37.9686
Alt3	37 54.9684	6 37.6824
Alt4	37 54.8508	6 37.2960
Alt5	37 54.7626	6 37.0680

23.
CORTELAZOR - CORTERRANGEL

Wp	N	W
1	37 56.1300	6 37.4868
2	37 56.1522	6 37.4082
3	37 56.1690	6 37.1484
4	37 56.1846	6 37.1148
5	37 56.2560	6 36.9672
6	37 56.2254	6 36.8736
7	37 56.2686	6 36.8112
8	37 56.2800	6 36.6144
9	37 56.2152	6 36.4932
10	37 56.2668	6 36.0480

24.
ALMONASTER CIRCULAR

Wp	N	W
1	37 52.4004	6 47.0334
2	37 52.4190	6 46.9452
3	37 52.4802	6 46.9524
4	37 52.5624	6 46.8552
5	37 52.6584	6 46.8870
6	37 52.8060	6 46.9752
7	37 52.8702	6 47.0334
8	37 52.9044	6 47.0814
9	37 52.9818	6 47.1180
10	37 53.1156	6 47.1894
11	37 53.2176	6 47.2488
12	37 53.1990	6 47.0874
13	37 53.2698	6 46.6650
14	37 53.1066	6 46.6650
15	37 53.0082	6 46.6386
16	37 53.1114	6 46.5762
17	37 53.2026	6 47.5380
18	37 53.2152	6 47.7624
19	37 53.3220	6 47.9130
20	37 53.4372	6 48.1020
21	37 53.5668	6 48.2808
22	37 53.3724	6 48.6114
23	37 53.3268	6 48.7650
24	37 53.1666	6 48.8400
25	37 52.9956	6 48.8508
26	37 52.9674	6 48.8256
27	37 52.9044	6 48.4104
28	37 52.7670	6 48.2130
29	37 52.7214	6 47.8776
30	37 52.6206	6 47.6562
31	37 52.4964	6 47.5218
32	37 52.4484	6 47.3838

25. CORTEGANA - LA POSADA CLASSIC

Wp	N	W
1	37 54.7182	6 49.1088
2	37 54.5946	6 49.1838
3	37 54.5352	6 49.1712
4	37 54.4608	6 49.0926
5	37 54.4956	6 48.9528
6	37 54.5034	6 48.8616
7	37 54.4308	6 48.7110
8	37 54.4434	6 48.6090
9	37 54.4038	6 48.5064
10	37 54.6108	6 48.3588
11	37 54.6948	6 48.2238
12	37 55.0980	6 48.2862
13	37 55.1250	6 48.3522
14	37 55.2060	6 48.3870
15	37 55.3554	6 48.4014
16	37 55.4598	6 48.3552
17	37 55.5612	6 48.3360
18	37 55.6836	6 48.3108
19	37 55.9146	6 48.2076
20	37 56.0244	6 48.2010
21	37 56.0376	6 48.1314

26. LA POSADA - CORTEGANA

Wp	N	W
1	37 56.0376	6 48.1314
2	37 56.0244	6 48.2010
3	37 55.9146	6 48.2076
4	37 55.7946	6 48.3048
5	37 55.7196	6 48.3996
6	37 55.6266	6 48.6504
7	37 55.6092	6 48.8994
8	37 55.5756	6 48.9840
9	37 55.4736	6 49.1568
10	37 55.4550	6 49.1868
11	37 55.3218	6 49.2240
12	37 55.1178	6 49.2666
13	37 55.1034	6 49.2348
14	37 54.9816	6 49.1748
15	37 54.9084	6 49.1184
16	37 54.8148	6 49.0560

27. CORTEGANA - LOS MOLINOS

Wp	N	W
1	37 54.8190	6 49.0482
2	37 54.8496	6 48.9144
3	37 54.9174	6 48.8574
4	37 54.9894	6 48.7188
5	37 55.0032	6 48.6756
6	37 55.0422	6 48.5418
7	37 55.0890	6 48.5082
8	37 55.1286	6 48.3636

This glossary contains Spanish words found in the text (shown in *italics*), plus other local words that you may encounter.

a

abandonado	abandoned
abierto	open
acantilado	cliff
aceituna	olive
acequia	water canal
acueducto	aqueduct
agua	water
agua no potable	water (not drinkable)
agua potable	drinking water
alcornoque	cork oak
aldea	hamlet, small village
aljibe	sunken water tank
alto	high
apaño	annual gathering of chestnuts
aparcamiento	parking
arroyo	stream
atajo	short cut
ayuntamiento	town hall

b

bajo	low
banco	bank
barranco	ravine
bellota	acorn
bocadillo	bread roll
bodegón	inn
bosque	wood, forest
cabra	goat

c

café	coffee
calle	street
camino	trail, path, track
camino particular	private road
camino real	old donkey trail (lit. royal road)
carne	meat
carretera	main road
carril	lane
casa	house
casa rural	country house accommodation to let
cascada	waterfall
caserío	hamlet, village
castaña	chestnut
castaño	chestnut tree
castillo	castle
cementerio	cemetery
cerdo ibérico	Iberian pig
cerrado	closed

cerveza (caña, jarra, presión, lata)	beer (small, large, draught, can)
choza	shelter
clinica	clinic, hospital
colmena	bee hive
comida	food
communidad	community
cordillera	mountain range
correos	post office
cortijo	farmstead
coto privado de caza	private hunting area
Cruz Roja	Red Cross (medical aid)
cuesta	slope
cumbre	peak, summit
cueva	cave
cumbre	summit

d

degollado	pass
dehesa	pasture
derecha	right (direction)
desayuno	breakfast
despejado	clear, fine
desprendimiento	landslide

e

embutido	sausage
encina	holm oak
ermita	chapel
este	east

f

farmacia	chemist
feria	country show, fair
fiesta	holiday, celebration
finca	farm, country house
fuente	fountain, public water supply

g

ganado	cattle
gasolinera	petrol station
Guardia Civil	police
guia	guide
GR (gran recorrido)	long distance walking route

h

horno de cal	lime kiln
hostal	hostel, accommodation
hoya	depression (geological)
huerta	smallholding, vegetable/fruit plot

huevos	eggs
i	
iglesia	church
información	information
invierno	winter
izquierda	left (direction)
j	
jamón	ham
l	
lavadero	public laundry area
librería	bookshop
llano	plain
lluvia, lluvioso	rain, rainy
lomo	broad-backed ridge
m	
mapa	map
manantial	spring
mercado	market
mirador	lookout/viewing point
molino	mill
montaña	mountain
museo	museum
musulmán	Moslem
n	
nieve	snow
norte	north
nublado	cloudy
o	
oeste	west
oficina de turísmo	tourist office
olivo	olive tree
otoño	autumn
oveja	sheep
p	
panadería	bakery
Paperos	Inhabitant of Fuentheridos (lit. potato people)
pastelería	cake shop
pata negra	the ham of the region (lit. black paw)
peligro	danger
pensión	guesthouse
PR (pequeño recorrido	short walking route
pescado	fish
pico	peak
pista	dirt road/track
pista (forestal)	forest road/track
playa	beach
plaza	square
plaza de toros	bullring
poblado	village
pocilga	pigsty
policia	police
posada	lodgings, hotel
postre	dessert
pozo	well
primavera	spring

prohibido el paso	no entry
pueblo	town, village
puente	bridge
puerto	port, mountain pass
q	
quercus	oak
queso	cheese
r	
retema	broom (botanical)
río	river
risco	cliff
roble	oak
roque	rock
ruta	route
s	
salida	exit
senda	path, track
sendero	foot path
setas	mushrooms
sierra	mountain range
sin salida	no through road/route no exit
sol	sun
sur	south
t	
tapas	bar snacks
té	tea
tiempo	weather
tienda	shop
tipico	traditional bar/eating place
tormenta	storm
tormentoso	stormy
toro	bull
torre	tower
tostados	chunky toast served at breakfast
tubería	water pipe
v	
vacuno(a)	cow
valle	valley
vega	meadow
ventoso	windy
verano	summer
vino (blanco, tinto, rosado)	wine (white, red, rosé)
z	
zona recreativa	recreation area
zumo/zumería	freshly pressed fruit juice/juice bar

Please note:

Telephone numbers are shown in red, and fax numbers in blue, and we show the entire number you need to dial from outside Spain. From within Spain, omit the 00 34.

ACCOMMODATION

Our list includes hotels, *pensiónes*, *posadas*, *casas rurales* and camp sites. We've stayed in four of them during the course of our research:

Hostal El Cruce (Santa Ana la Real)
We've stayed at this family-run crossroads hostel on the junction of the N 435 and A 470 three times. The rooms are clean, basic and a bit cramped, and it was quite noisy the last time we stayed. There's a good atmosphere in the bar where you can partake of a basic breakfast of coffee and *tostados* with jam, honey, paté or olive oil. There's a restaurant attached, although as is usual in Spain away from tourist areas, you won't find them serving until around ten in the evening. Plenty of parking, inexpensive, though you need good Spanish.

Hotel Sierra de Aracena (Aracena)
There's an air of faded gentility about this two star establishment in a good location for exploring the main town of the region, and with a reasonable choice of eating and drinking places within a few minutes walk. Breakfasts consist of the ubiquitous doorsteps of toast, as well as biscuits, cakes, yoghurt and fruit. Street parking only, which can be tricky at weekends and whenever there's a *fiesta* or special event in town.

Villa Turística de Fuenteheridos (Fuenteheridos)
A perfect location below the little town of **Fuenteheridos**, you have an entire terraced house to yourself, with grazing sheep on your front doorstep. You get plenty of room (separate lounge, own garden, large bathroom, log stove, heating/air conditioning, kitchen area). Minus points; there's not so much as a teaspoon in the kitchen - fine if you live in Seville and can pack everything in the boot, but tricky for those flying in with a meagre baggage allowance. Room prices include a full buffet breakfast - do insist on this, as if they are nearly empty they tend to 'forget'. Don't bother with the evening meals - far better to go into **Fuenteheridos**.

Hotel Galaroza Sierra (Galaroza)
This two star hotel is in ideally located for several of our routes. Once up its steep driveway and climb to the front door, it is comfortable and well-run if a little lacking in personality.

ALÁJAR (post code 21340)

Molino Río Alájar	00 34 959 501282/3	00 34 959 125766
Casas Rurales	rioalajar@wanadoo.es	
Finca Cabeza del Molino	www.molinorioalajar.com	

La Posada
Hotel-Restaurant*
Calle Médico E González, 2

00 34 959 125712

00 34 959 125712

ALMONASTER LA REAL (post code 21350)

Casa García
Hotel-Restaurant**
Avda. San Martín, 2
(22 rooms)

00 34 959 143109

00 34 959 143143

Posada el Camino
Hotel-Restaurant
Cortegana - Aracena road km 6.8
(10 rooms)

00 34 959 503240
www.posadaelcamino.com

Finca los Gallos
Casas Rurales
Estación de Almonaster
(3km north of town, towards Cortegana)

00 34 959 501167
www.alojamientolosgallos.com

La Cruz
Hostel-Restaurant*
Plaza de los Llanos, 8

00 34 959 143135

ARACENA (post code 21200)

Sierra de Aracena
Hotel**
Gran Vía, 21
(42 rooms)

00 34 959 126175

00 34 959 126281

Finca Valbono
Hotel* & Casas Rurales**
Carboneras road km 1
Hotel, & 20 cottages

00 34 959 127711

00 34 959 127679 6

Los Castaños
Hotel-Restaurant**
Avenida de Huelva, 5

00 34 959 126300

00 34 959 126287

Camping Aracena Sierra
Campsite
N 433 km 83

00 34 959 501005
fontanil@hotmail.com

00 34 959 536237

Casa Manolo
Pension
Barberos, 6

00 34 959 128014

CORTECONCEPCIÓN

La Casa del Cura
Hostel-Restaurant
Calle Iglesia, 10

00 34 959 120120

La Barcina
Hostel-Restaurant
Avenida de la Diputación

00 34 959 120120

CORTEGANA (post code 21230)

La Posada de Cortegana
Rural Hotel-Restaurant**
El Repilado - La Corte
road km 2.5

00 34 959 503301/17
00 34 959 503356/02
hotel_laposada@terra.es
www.posadadecortegana.com

Cervantes
Pension*
Calle Cervantes, 27

00 34 959 131592

CORTELAZOR

El Precio Justo
Casa Rural
Carretera Los Marines - Cortelazor km 2

00 34 959 126072

FUENTEHERIDOS (post code 21292)

Finca el Moro
Casas Rurales
walking & riding holidays
(contact Nick Tudor)

00 34 959 50107   00 34 959 501092
fincaelmoro@telefonica.net
www.fincaelmoro.com

Villa Turística de
Fuenteheridos
Rural Hotel***
N 433 km 97
(41 villas)

00 34 959 125202   00 34 959 125199
vtfuenteheridos.reservas@fp-hoteles.com
www.fp-hoteles.com

Camping El Madroñal
Campsite & cabins
Fuenteheridos - Castaño del Robledo road km 0.6

00 34 959 501200

Carballo
Pension*
Calle La Fuente, 16

00 34 959 125108

GALAROZA (post code 21291)

Galaroza Sierra
Hotel-Restaurant**
N 433 km 69.5

00 34 959 123237   00 34 959 123236
informacion@hotelgalaroza.com
www.hotelgalaroza.com

Hostal Venecia
Hostel-Restaurant* N 433

00 34 959 123098

Toribio
Pension
Calle Iglesia, 11

00 34 959 123073

JABUGO (post code 21290)

La Silladilla	00 34 959 501350	00 34 959 501351
Hotel****	silladi@teleline.es	
Los Romeros	www.jabugo.cc	

Aurora   00 34 959 121146
Pension*
Calle Barco, 9

LOS MARINES (post code 21208)

Finca del Buenvino	00 34 959 124034	00 34 959 501029
Bed & Breakfast Inn	availability@fincabuenvino.com	
N 433 km 95	www.fincabuenvino.com	

SANTA ANA LA REAL

El Cruce   00 34 959 122333/501153
Hostal-Restaurant*
N 435/A470 crossroads

Gruta de las Maravillas
Caves and subterranean lakes
Pozo de la Nieve   00 34 959 128355   00 34 959 128206
Aracena 21200

Centro de Vistantes   00 34 959 128825
Visitors' Centre/Tourist Information
Cabildo Viejo   www.cma.junta-andalucia.es
Plaza Alta
Aracena 21200

Embalse de Aracena (Reservoir of Aracena), NE of Aracena on the HV 3116

Tren Turístico   00 34 959 127045/514   00 34 959 128825
Tourist 'train' ride   www.cma.junta-andalucia.es
Cabildo Viejo (bookings)
Plaza Alta
Aracena 21200   (Leaves from Plaza de San Pedro)

Museo Minero-Geológico
Geology and Mining Museum
Plaza de San Pedro   00 34 959 128355
Aracena 21200

Museo del Jamón Ham Museum
Plaza de Doña Elvira
Aracena 21200

Jamones La Joya   00 34 959 126883
Gran Vía, 6
Aracena (Excellent ham & local produce shop, with bar)

Picadero La Suerte   00 34 959 123010   00 34 959 123367
Horse Riding   picad.lasuerte@terra.es
Finca La Suerte   www.fincalasuerte.com
Carril Cuesta Palero
Galaroza 21291

Finca el Moro   00 34 959 50107   00 34 959 501092
Casas Rurales   fincaelmoro@telefonica.net
walking & riding holidays www.fincaelmoro.com
(contact Nick Tudor)

Cinco Jotas   00 34 959 121076   00 34 959 121194
Ham Factory   jabugo@osborne.es
Carretera San Juán del Puerto
Jabugo 21290 (Tour of a ham factory)

Minas de Ríotinto   00 34 959 590025   00 34 959 591074
The mines, and Mining Museum
Plaza del Museo   aeg1657x@elsendero.es
Minas de Ríotinto 21660 www.aventuraminaparque.org

TOURIST INFORMATION

Punto de Información   00 34 959 143206
Tourist Information
Ayuntamiento
Almonaster la Real 21350

Centro de Visitantes   00 34 959 127045/514   00 34 959 128825
Parque Natural de Sierra de Aracena y Picos de Aroche
Cabildo Viejo
Plaza Alta   www.cma.junta-andalucia.es
Aracena 21200

Centro de Turísmo   00 34 959 128355   00 34 959 128206
Rural Tourist Information & Booking Office
Calle Poza de la Nieve
Aracena 21200

Punto de Información   00 34 959 503054
Tourist Information
Castillo de Cortegana
Cortegana 21230

 Emergency number (equivalent of 999) 112

 Taxi (note - these are extremely scarce, and you'll normally need to book in advance)   959 128429   617 422003(mobile)

🍽 RESTAURANTS & BARS

There are scores of these, so we mention only those we've personally tried and can recommend, plus a couple that have earned their place here by reputation. We do name others in the walk descriptions, usually because they are in the right location, and not because they offer culinary excellence.

Mesón el Corcho   00 34 959 125779
Restaurant/unofficial cork museum
Plaza de España, 3
Alájar 21340
We would have included this restaurant, even if the food had been mediocre which it certainly is not. Recommended for food, service and the unique setting. See Walk 10, and the section on **Alájar** in the introduction.

José Vicente Restaurant   00 34 959 128455
Avenida Andalucía, 53
Aracena 21200
This restaurant has a formidable reputation. Recommended by Geoff Garvey of Rough Guides, and booking is advisable. Specialises in *jamón serrano*.

Café Bar Manzano
Plaza Marqués de Aracena
Aracena 21200
Popular, atmospheric meeting place with tables in and outside in Aracena's central square. Quick service by slick waiters. Ideal for just a drink or something more substantial.

El Diablo Bar/Restaurant
Plaza Coso
Fuenteheridos 21295
Favourite place for locals and visitors to congregate. Excellent ham, eggs and chips. Shows important televised sports fixtures.

Aguafría
on the N435 main road
Small stylish country restaurant with extensive local menu plus snacks. Recommended for late upmarket lunch or dinner.

Swifty's Lunchtime Diner
N433 km 105 (opposite the petrol station)
Jabugo (nearest town)

You are likely to dismiss this unusual, and completely unpretentious, local diner as you speed along the N433. Looking like an army surplus greenhouse, **Swifty's** (not its name, but so-called by us in the apparent absence of an official one) offers a good value, hearty lunch for €8 including a drink. Immaculate owner and waiter contrast with the basic decor of calendars from local businesses. Every day there is a wide choice of starters and main courses but no menu; they read the choices to you rapidly (in Spanish) and after choosing drinks and first course rapidly arrive, following service is equally swift - hence our name. Recommended; any *revueltas* starter and fresh fish main course. You just can't say that you have 'eaten locally' without at least one visit to **Swifty's**. Open 11.00 to 15.00 daily.

Mesón Arrieros 00 34 959 463715
Restaurant
Calle Arrieros
Linares de la Sierra
Has a good reputation as a fine restaurant serving local specialties.

 WEBSITES

Search the web using 'Sierra de Aracena' and you'll find lots of sites, although many of them are in Spanish. If you want to look for accommodation, then you'll find a number of websites to whet your appetite. There are also a few tour operator and walking holiday sites. Please note that we have not repeated websites and/or email contacts already mentioned elsewhere in these appendices.

Some of the following are 'official' sites run by town councils or government/regional tourist departments, while others are commercial ventures offering good information, while advertising their accommodation to rent.

www.andalucia.com

www.almonasterlareal.com

www.fuenteheridos.com

www.jamondehuelva.com

www.andalucia-web.net

www.sol.com

www.spainatheart.co.uk

www.spainview.com

www.oleonline.com

www.cortegana.com

www.diphuelva.es

www.sierradearacena.net

www.juntadeandalucia.es

www.andalusia-web.com

www.toprural.com

Maps

Two Spanish organisations publish the closest equivalents to traditional Ordnance Survey style maps. They are:-

Centro Nacional de Información Geográfica
Oficina Central, Monte Esquinza, 41
28010 Madrid, Spain
Tel: 00 34 91 5979453   Fax: 00 34 91 5532913
www.cnig.es   consulta@cnig.es.

Servicio Geográfico del Ejército
Dario Gazapo, 8
28024 Madrid, Spain
Tel: 00 34 91 7115043   Fax: 00 34 91 7115033

Sierra de Aracena Tour & Trail Map 1:40,000 scale by David & Ros Brawn (Pub. Discovery Walking Guides Ltd. 2004) £2.99 **ISBN 1-899554-97-1** Clear, detailed, up to date, indispensable

Sierra de Aracena y Pícos de Aroche (Pub. Instituto de Cartografía de Andalucía 1998) 1:75,000 scale. Large, unwieldy and not very useful. This map and the following one may be on sale in the **Tourist Office** in **Aracena**.

Mapa Guía de Sierra de Aracena y Pícos de Aroche (Pub. Ayuntamiento de Aracena 2002) €4.50 1:100,000 scale with an area expanded to 1:60,000 scale. Walking information (in Spanish) and some routes marked, though not all are passable. Sketch maps of town and village streets.

Books

There are very few publications specifically for the Sierra de Aracena, though some books on Andalucía or southern Spain include a section on the region. Bookshops are rare once you get here, so best to buy ahead. Some of the more obscure titles listed below may be hard to track down, but most are listed on amazon.co.uk

Walking Books & Information

Walking in Andalucía by Guy Hunter-Watts (Pub. Santana Ediciones SL) £14.00 **ISBN 8-489954-24-0**
Covers all of Andalucía, with just a couple of routes in the Sierra de Aracena. Now rather out of date.

Parque Natural, Sierra de Aracena y Picos de Aroche (Guías Verde, Pub. Susaeta Ediciones SA) **ISBN 8-430586-36-9**
N.B In Spanish, though a good source of background detail. Includes itineraries by car and some suitable for bicycle/on foot.

Ask in the **Tourist Office** in **Aracena** near the entrance to the **Gruta de las Maravillas**, and in the **Centro de Visitantes** in Plaza Alta, **Aracena** for current local information and maps produced by the Local Government.

General, Background & Reference Books

Rough Guide to Andalucía by Mark Ellingham and Geoff Garvey (Pub. Rough Guides, part of Penguin) £10.99 **ISBN 1-843530-68-6**
Usual fact-packed tome we've all come to expect from Rough Guides, with about ten pages on the region of Sierra de Aracena.

Andalucía by John Noble, Susan Forsyth and Des Hannigan (Pub. Lonely Planet 2003) £10.99 **ISBN 1-740592-79-4**

Andalus - Unlocking the Secrets of Moorish Spain (Doubleday) £12.99 **ISBN 0-385605-07-2**

La Vida Rural en La Sierra de Huelva by Manuel Moreno Alonso (Pub. Instituto de Estudios Onubenses 1979) **ISBN 8-400044-46-0**
N.B. In Spanish only

Historia de la Arquitectura Inglesa en Huelva by Miguel González Vilchez (Pub. Diputación Provincial de Huelva 2000) **ISBN 8-447206-06-8**
N.B. In Spanish only

Not on Queen Victoria's Birthday - The Story of the Río Tinto Mines by David Avery (Collins 1974) £29.95 **ISBN 0-002113-34-1**

Benito Arias Montano (Pub. Warburg Institute 1992) £5
ISBN 0-854810-46-3

Where to Watch Birds in Southern and Western Spain by Ernest García and Andrew Patterson (Pub. Christopher Helm 2001) £33.98
ISBN 0-713653-01-9

A Selection of Wildflowers of Southern Spain by Betty Allen (Santana Ediciones SL) £12.50 **ISBN 8-489954-12-7**

Field Guide to Wild Flowers of Southern Europe by Paul Davies and Bob Gibbons (Pub. Crowood Press Ltd. 1993) £10.99 **ISBN 1-852236-59-0**

Magazine

Entorno Natural Magazine of Rural Tourism
First published in April 2004, this Spanish-English magazine is attractive if a bit thin on content, though may develop as it matures. Ask in the Tourist Office in **Aracena**.

Sierra de Aracena

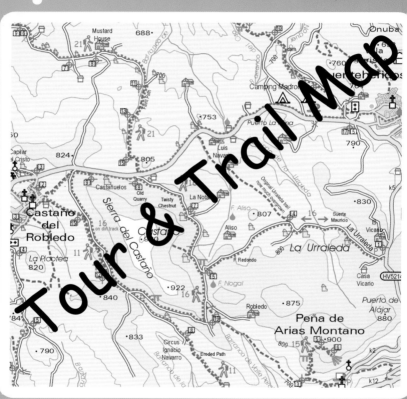

Tour & Trail Map

Fully Detailed 1:40,000 Scale Map

£2.99 UK / €4.50 EU

Discovery Walking Guides Ltd
ISBN 1-899554-97-1
Copyright David & Ros Brawn

9 781899 554973

Tour & Trail Maps have been developed to meet the need for accurate, up to date, maps for regions covered by Discovery Walking Guides. At the core of each T&T map design is a comprehensive ground-level survey carried out on foot and by car. The survey results are then translated into our design programme, producing a digital vector-graphic database involving the organisation of several million pieces of information across a large number of 'layers' drawn digitally within our computers.

Once a digital vector-graphic database has been established, new developments such as new roads, tracks and buildings, can be quickly incorporated into the correct 'layer' of the database. Rapid updating, combined with state of the art 'file to plate' pre-press operation enables us to produce new editions of Tour & Trail Maps quickly and efficiently.

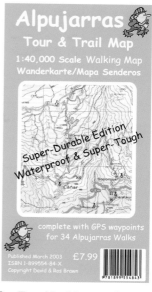

Alpujarras Tour & Trail Map — 1:40,000 Scale Walking Map — Wanderkarte/Mapa Senderos — Super-Durable Edition Waterproof & Super-Tough — complete with GPS waypoints for 34 Alpujarras Walks — Published March 2003 — ISBN 1-899554-84-X — Copyright David & Ros Brown — £7.99

Tour & Trail Maps have Latitude/Longitude grids and datum information making them GPS compatible. DWG walking routes are clearly highlighted, along with their GPS Waypoints where space allows.

Since 2003, all new Tour & Trail Maps have been produced on a special high density polymer as Super-Durable editions which are waterproof and super tough, giving many seasons of use in the toughest conditions and outlasting paper maps many times over.

Mallorca North & Mountains Tour & Trail Map — 1:40,000 Scale — Super-Durable Edition Waterproof & Super-Tough — Fully Updated 3rd Edition on Super-Durable polymer — £7.99 UK / €11.50 Mallorca — Discovery Walking Guides Ltd — ISBN 1-899554-93-9 — Copyright David & Ros Brown

Tour & Trail Maps are available for:-
La Gomera
Alpujarras
Madeira
Mallorca North & Mountains
Menorca
Gran Canaria Mountains

Tenerife Walkers' Maps are available in both paper & Super-Durable editions.

Sierra de Aracena Tour & Trail Map £2.99 isbn 1-899554-97-1 is printed on a 115gsm specialist map paper

Spending a lot of our time amongst dramatic landscapes, we appreciate the value of an accurately researched and well written walk description. Abroad in a foreign land is no place to find yourself lost and in danger. Knowing this, we operate a 'no compromise' policy to all of DWG's walking routes. We walk every route - repeatedly if necessary - to make sure that we have an accurate walk description. Then we try to write the detailed walk description in an inspirational tone so that you know how we felt on that route. We've slogged up that impossible looking ascent, marvelled at those panoramas, found paths through apparently pathless wilderness, have gratefully arrived at our destination. It's not always fun, but it has always been an adventure. Our GPS ground survey system means that we know exactly where we have been, except when there is poor GPS reception and we tell you this.

This 'no compromise' policy for our walking research has been much appreciated by users of DWG walking guides, as our post bag testifies. This means that with a DWG guidebook, you can confidently embark on the adventures it contains, knowing that we've researched every route to the highest standard.

We still marvel at every 'Your guide made my holiday' letter we receive, just as we did at the first one we ever received. Bringing adventure and enjoyment to people is very pleasing, and we are very good listeners to what our readers would like to appear in a walk description.

In Sierra de Aracena - a Walk! Guidebook you'll find:-

- Walking route summary including Effort, Time, Distance, Ascents/Descents, and Refreshments
- Frequent timings so that you can judge your progress against ourselves
- Fully detailed walk description
- Detailed map for every walking route
- GPS Waypoints (grid references) for every key point on the route
- Full GPS Waypoint lists for all walking routes
- National and regional Locator maps
- lots of useful background information

We haven't done all this just because the Sierra de Aracena is somewhere special, which it certainly is; this is our normal 'no compromise' approach to giving you everything you need in a walking guide book. Now, go out there and enjoy it, safe in the knowledge that we have been there before and we have a full GPS track and waypoint record of where we've been. Generally our routes are straightforward, so long as you follow the walk descriptions; some routes have many potentially confusing junctions. While many of our routes are linear, we have grouped them together matrix fashion so that you can easily combine routes into 'full day' circular walks. All that is necessary is for you to get out there, marvelling at the beautiful landscapes, ancient towns with their marble cobbled streets, the amazing flora and fauna, enjoying 'ham, egg & chips' in El Diablo, plus masses of new discoveries.

David & Ros Brawn
Directors of Discovery Walking Guides Ltd
(That's us in some of the Walk photographs)